G.O.D.

by Amy Nanette Glin

© 2024 Amy Nanette Glin

ISBN: 979-8-9900436-0-2

Edited by: Susan Uttendorfsky, Adirondack Editing
Cover Design: Diren Yardimli, BookCoverZone
Layout by: Susan Uttendorfsky, Adirondack Editing

DEDICATION

This book is dedicated to:

Plants
Animals
Air
Water
Fire
Earth
The Field
and
Human Beings
everywhere

And to SpirIT, the ultimate tuner.

"The conscious and intelligent manipulation of the organized habits and opinions of the masses is an important element in democratic society. Those who manipulate this unseen mechanism of society constitute an invisible government which is the true ruling power of our country.

"We are governed, our minds are molded, our tastes formed, our ideas suggested, largely by men we have never heard of. This is a logical result of the way in which our democratic society is organized. Vast numbers of human beings must cooperate in this manner if they are to live together as a smoothly functioning society...

"...whatever attitude one chooses to take toward this condition, it remains a fact that in almost every act of our daily lives, whether in the sphere of politics or business, in our social conduct or our ethical thinking, we are dominated by the relatively small number of persons—a trifling fraction of our hundred and twenty million—who understand the mental processes and social patterns of the masses. It is they who pull the wires which control the public mind, who harness old social forces and contrive new ways to bind and guide the world."

Edward Bernays, *Propaganda*, 1928[1]

But not for much longer...

---

[1] Historyisaweapon.com
An aside: Edward Bernays was Sigmund Freud's nephew.

A long time ago, farther back than you can remember...

SpirIT of G.O.D. and Lucifer of E.G.O. wagered a little bet that commenced the longest game of Earthopoly ever played—as well as the most important.

This game isn't for property, but for souls.

When Earth year 2030 ends, whoever has the most dedicated souls on their side gains jurisdiction of planet Earth indefinitely.

The future of the planet... Prison or Prism?

Who will have your soul when the curtains are drawn?

PART ONE

one

I am there, but I don't remember much. My newly opened eyes can't comprehend the gravity of what just happened. After squeezing through that dark tunnel and bursting into light, strange creatures abound, along with the brightness and the funny sounds, including the words, "It's a beautiful baby girl!"

I'm whisked into a small box with a light. "She's a little small," someone says. "She arrived early." That's the beginning of my contradiction—arriving early at a place I don't want to be.

And I've heard stories about those times. About two weeks later, my mother carries me out of the building, gets into a taxicab, and, while sobbing, hands me over to something called "a lawyer." Three weeks old and I already know what it feels like to want a shower after meeting someone.

I'm taken on a ride that ends when the lawyer hands me over to my new mother, a soon-to-be divorced woman hellbent on having a target for her boundless anger at her cheating husband, whom she's convinced is my biological father. Twice delivered.

My first memory is somewhere between four and six years old. I'm playing hide and seek with my best friend Craig in the empty lot next to my house. A tree sticks out its root and trips me, causing my little body to hit the ground with great force. Wracked with pain, I manage to hold back my tears so I can stay hidden.

I take my commitments very seriously.

Even at five. Even in fun.

Craig finds me pretty quickly and when he does, I burst into tears. He has no idea what happened, why I'm crying, or how to help me. It's probably one of his first experiences of not understanding women. I can't talk; I'm in too much pain to explain. Tears stream down my face. Together we walk to the sidewalk in front of my house and I sit down on the warm cement slab.

By this time, I'm crying so hard that I'm gasping for air in between sobs. Craig, seemingly traumatized himself, turns his back and walks home, leaving me sitting there…by myself…sobbing. Boys.

My mother isn't home, so Liz, our housekeeper/nanny, calls her. It isn't as chichi as it sounds. My mother and father have long ago divorced and my mother works full time. Someone has to watch the children—my brother and me. Liz came our way via a phone call to a wrong number: "You wanna talk to who? … You're looking for what? … No one here by that name, but I need a job." The background check consisted of "What time can you come over?" Fortunately for us all, it worked out.

My mother, upset that she has to leave work because of me, picks me up in our big black Chevy Impala and races to the Emergency Room, all the way telling me to stop crying. I try, but I'm in more pain than ever before. We wait for what seems like hours and finally get called in. The doctor lifts me up on the examining table.

All of a sudden, something occurs that feels, oddly, both uncomfortable and normal. As I'm being examined, I'm simultaneously watching him examine me from above. In both places at the same time. I can't tell anyone, because besides not knowing how to describe what's happening, I have a difficult enough time being heard by the adults in my life about things I can explain.

Diagnosis? Broken collarbone. Nothing can be done except to put my arm in a sling…and give my mother some tranquilizers. I rejoin myself, merging the above-who-sees with the below-that-feels and go home with my somewhat-apologetic mother. We stop for ice cream.

Sometime during the next week, I find myself wondering about what happened at the hospital, which leads me to deeper thoughts. How was I looking down at myself on that table? And from where? I get curious and start questioning, *What was I before I became me?*

Every day, I sit with my fists clenched and my brow furrowed, desperately trying to grasp onto an inkling of information about what happened in the Emergency Room and how this cosmic container for life really works. Contracting my whole body, trying with all my might to open up to the flow of wisdom doesn't work. Nothing does.

Before giving up, I make a solemn vow. Well, two. One, regain that wisdom and bring it forth. The other? Maintain access to the information for eternity.

Tall order for a short five-year-old from the suburbs.

two

It's thirty-nine years later... I'm forty-four as I examine my lined face in the bathroom mirror. After spending tens of thousands of dollars and countless hours attending seminars, reading self-help books, going to therapists, and trying every new, old, and repackaged method for coming to terms with being alive, I still live on the fence of existence. I don't understand cheery people who never stop blabbing about how "life is a gift."

Shut the fuck up. Life's a sentence!

"Shit, I'm late," I shout, running out the door.

Even after endless hours of self-examination, aura clearings, and trying nearly every newfound voodoo, woo-woo method of getting happy, the truth is that I still find myself angry much of the time.

Whizzing off in my old faithful Toyota Camry, I ponder...

I don't even know who to be pissed off at! God? Politicians? The asshole driving in front of me who's on the phone, putting on makeup, and giving *ME* the finger? My mother? My father? And which one, to boot—biological, adopted, or step? Trust me, I have a case for everything and everyone mentioned.

For as long as I can remember, I've wondered what I did wrong to deserve coming back here again—I know for a fact I was sent down the wrong chute. *Get me the manager of earthly incarnations NOW!!* I laugh at the irony as a laundry truck passes me. *Wrong chute, right!*

Strangely enough, this approach hasn't worked. Up until now, I haven't been successful in commanding the universe to answer to my whims, so I've decided it's time to take a new tack. If I'm not going to end my life, things have to change. I must allow something to dislodge my indignity. It's time to give up disdain at being in a body in exchange for acceptance and awe of the great mystery, *el misterio*. Life.

Okay, I'm ready.

Since I'll be turning forty-five soon—about the halfway point, I figure—I've decided to enter the second part of my life unencumbered. It's time to get happy.

In the elevator, I make a pact with myself to finally accept life. Any thoughts, ways of being, belief systems, habits, relationships—any patterns that stop me from being able to process my feelings about myself, others, and being alive—will be changing.

Entering my acupuncturist's office, I mutter to myself, "I'm opening a new book and shedding the actions that keep me bound to a dysfunctional past to make room for a fully functional future."

Determined to recognize myself as vital—and as important as anyone else on this planet—I give myself the thirty days before my birthday to clean up that past just as Craig, my acupuncturist, waves me in.

Another tall order. I seem to be fond of them.

"We've got a lot of work to do," I tell him as he hands me a cup of tea.

three

CPR[2] is always busy, and this moment's no different. Even at five a.m., the control room is hopping. Worker and Messenger angels dash back and forth. There's much to do. Prayer requests coming from Earth have reached an alarming number—all hands are called on deck to help with the onslaught.

Lord senses the commotion and floats in to see what the fuss is all about. Able to appear in any shape or size, one never knows how Lord's going to show up. Today, like most days, his chosen form is that of a modern-day sage: marvelously flamboyant and ageless, dressed in a red robe with red hair to match. Lord loves color, both visually and when demonstrated in souls.

He's singing one of his favorite James Brown tunes, "It's a Man's World," and croons the line about women.

CPR, with all its activities and workers, is quite colorful, too. The room glows ice-blue, reflecting universal hues from the large picture windows. Lord appears simply vibrant against that background. Collectively, the angels' movements create rainbows across the space. In the lower ranks, each angel displays a color identifying their level of advancement on the wheel of life. In the upper ranks, they grow wings.

Gabriel's hazel eyes beam as he rushes to Lord.

"Earthlings are troubled more than usual this week," G.O.D.'s Chief of Programming exclaims. "Prayer requests

---

[2] Center Presenting Reality ~ Headquarters of G.O.D. (Galactic Order of Demonstration).

sextuple daily! Souls have forgotten their own inner powers, they're—"

"Beseeching us to do their work for them?" Lord raises an eyebrow.

"No. It's as if they're hypnotized. They don't seem to remember that demonstration is the only prayer, and that accepting and using their gifts is the ultimate expression. They're not seeking out the built-in clues for soul advancement, or using the laws to work with The Field."[3]

"Time spent on Earth was supposed to be an interactive adventure..." Lord sounds perplexed. "It's mind-boggling that earthlings aren't transceiving[4] with The Field. This makes no sense."

"They waste so much energy on wishing and hoping for things to be better when it could be used for uncovering clues to advancement and demonstrating their own inner knowings."[5] Gabe's strong features fall into disappointment. "I've been contemplating ways to pull them out of their daze. Drastic action is in order. We need to wake them up! So many prayer requests coming in." He shakes his head. "So much energy wasted."

"The law of ASK/GET has been misunderstood." Lord generates a dove out of thin air as he speaks. "It's not an invitation for them to request that the universe bend to their will."

"ASK/GET is an invitation to Always Seek Knowing/ Gain Eternal Truths," Gabe says. "That's how I remember it."

---

[3] The Field: The interactive container we live in. Frequency In Earth's Linear Dimension.

[4] A transceiver has the circuitry to both transmit and receive. Earthlings are transceivers.

[5] Innate, intuitive knowledge that doesn't have to be learned.

"Beautiful. That is now the official definition! Things are at a boiling point on Spaceship Earth, and rightfully so. Earthlings trapped in E.G.O.'s web will not accept change unless staying the same is more painful than doing something about it."

Lord's forehead wrinkles. "But I'm perplexed. Are they really so dense? The funny thing is, prayers executed in this manner have never worked. They just keep doing the same thing over and over again and expecting different results."

"Ahh, yes. It's called the Moron Syndrome." Gabriel chuckles. "But sometimes it appears to work; that's why they believe in praying so strongly. And it seems only a handful of them understand the way the place really operates."

"Interesting."

"Perhaps they're confusing the confirmation they receive from demonstrating their understanding of Universal laws with prayers being answered?" Gabe gazes out the window. "*Something* isn't right."

"It must have to do with the bet. I'm not sure how Cretin has tricked so many into believing in this 'God who answers prayers' that he promotes. The truth of the game of life on Earth is so much more extraordinary than deferring to some invisible being in the sky for needs and wants. Earthlings have so much power within themselves."

"It was spelled out in the **H**eaven **O**n **M**other **E**arth Law Book." Gabe shakes his head. "People aren't following it, though. I don't understand."

"HOME is our greatest gift to earthly incarnates in the history of creation. It outlines the fantastic journey that is life on Earth. I don't get it either," Lord says. "Convene a meeting with my son and your four best angels. Include Michael. It's time to discuss the plan for Earth's wake-up call."

"We have a plan?" Gabe's eyes sparkle.

Suddenly, a woman's voice floats in...

"Grrrrr. I demand sleep, and I demand it NOW! What do you need, some goddamned gratitude to grant my request? Well, thank you very much."

They note there's no *please*, no *thank you*—just *do it*.

"What do you need so much admiration for anyway? A real God could exist without a constant need for gratitude and recognition. You're great. You're da bomb. Okay? I need SLEEP. Put me out. Please!"

The voice trickles off.

"Whew," Gabriel replies. "Someone down there has clearly had it."

"That sounded like Nanette. Call the meeting," Lord orders. "This is the time we have been waiting for. We will meet in the conference room."

Gabe, anxious to hear what Lord has to say, darts out of the room as Lord's son, Chip, saunters in, looking like he just woke up. In fact, he did, and his sweet boyish face is still a bit wrinkled. But with a three-day beard growth, Chip's a sight to behold. Angels swoon as he passes, filling the room with green and orange hues. He activates their second and fourth chakras[6] and the energy spills out everywhere.

"Don't bother shaving for us," Lord teases, knowing Chip has always preferred a casual style, even when he lived on Earth as Jesus.

Chip laughs. It's always wise to laugh at Lord's jokes.

---

[6] Chakras are energy centers, or portals, in the human energy field. Located along the central line of the body, from the base of the spine to the top of the head, they are conceived of as whirling, wheel-like vortices through which universal/cosmic energy flows into and out of a person. There are seven major chakras, plus many minor ones. Each corresponds to specific glands, organs, and facets of your being. "Seven Chakra Charts: The Basics You Need To Know About The Chakras," The Energy Healing Site.

Together they head over to the conference room. It's already set up with tea and water, and berries and clotted cream. There is also fresh-squeezed grapefruit juice, Lord's favorite. He pours them both a glass before he sits down.

Chip takes a sip. He sits down, and then stands up again. "Father, I've just woken from a dream—E.G.O. won control of the planet by infiltrating every avenue of information. Their tactics hurt everyone and everything, including man, animals, the planet itself, and all her systems. Men and women became miserable and started rebelling."

"You have always been a prophetic dreamer, son."

Chip paces back and forth in front of Lord. He stops before him, puts his right hand on Lord's left shoulder, and looks him directly in the eye. "There's something I have to tell you."

Lord receives Chip's hand by placing his own on top of it. "Tell me, son, how has the Earth realm gotten so out of control? Why are souls not enamored by the inherent game that is life on Earth? The treasure hunt is designed to be so intriguing, empowering, and elegant. Perhaps E.G.O. might persuade a few souls with their antics, but they have no chance at claiming the majority. Oh, and don't forget fun. Life on Earth is supposed to be fun!"

Chip is now fully awake as his father continues. "I wonder if there is something I don't know." Chip begins pacing again as Lord muses, "Is it possible that even one with access to all knowledge and wisdom—me—doesn't know everything? SpirIT has always taught that it's more important to know what you don't know rather than what you do know. Hmmm. I guess the only way I'd know if there was something I didn't know was if there was something I didn't know. How can you know what you don't know? How do I know what—"

"Father! You're stuck in linear looping again. Demonstrate attunement!"

"Jesus, Chip. No need to bark."

"You were clearly stuck. Sometimes it takes a roar. And there *is* something I have to tell you. Something that will explain things."

"Thanks, my wise one. You are correct—demonstration is always key. At times even I have to be reminded that SpirIT is all-knowing and I am simply IT's[7] emissary," Lord admits. "I have to watch that…"

SpirIT invisibly pops in for a moment at the mention of IT's name. Known among colleagues simply as "IT," SpirIT provides tuning fodder[8] to every living thing in G.O.D., including Lord. IT's residence contains orchestras of the finest instruments ever to exist.

"It's easier than one thinks to get caught in a linear looping trap," Lord asserts, "but also easy to get out of—with tools and an understanding of the workings of The Field."

Chip's father waves his hand and a hamster running in a wheel appears on the table in front of them. With a nod to the rodent, its little paws stop.

Lord stands up. "You have to stop long enough to get off the wheel." The rodent steps down and squeals. The red-robed overseer tosses it a bit of apple, stretches, and brings himself to order.

"Ahh, yes… SpirIT, tools, and The Field. That's what I need to talk with you about. There *is* something you don't

---

[7] SpirIT's nickname, which stands for "I Tune."

[8] Any communication from SpirIT through The Field to earthlings that aligns them or offers them insights into the workings of the Earth plane. Tuning fodder can come from anywhere at any time, sometimes with significant impact. Communications can be in a song, a seeming chance overhearing of a relevant conversation, direct communications, "random" meaningful encounters, etc. It all has to do with timing, relevance, and reception. Listening and attention required.

know related to how Cretin and E.G.O. have gained so much control."

"I knew it!" Lord says. "Wait a minute… If I know I do not know something, do I know something or not know something?"

Chip is somber and not playing into Lord's game at the moment. "That's the eternal paradox, isn't it, Father?"

"Sorry, son. What is it you want to tell me?"

"Something that you're not going to enjoy hearing very much. Sit down, Pop. Remember, love is inherently unconditional, okay?"

Lord's eyes lock on Chip.

A bit of sweat drips down the side of his face. "I know why Cretin appears to be winning…"

Gabriel bounds into the conference room. "The angels will be right here—"

"Sorry, Gabe." Lord gives him the hand. "Give us a couple of minutes. Chip was just telling me something privately."

He nods and steps out.

"Okay, here goes." Chip pours himself a glass of ice water and takes a sip. "You know the Law Book?"

"You mean HOME? What about it?"

"It didn't get distributed. Earthlings never received the laws of their dimension…or the overstandings[9] necessary to elevate themselves to human beings." Chip swallows. "It's why men and women still get excited when synchronicity happens rather than become concerned when it doesn't."

His father's face now matches his red hair and frock.

---

[9] Overstanding is being privy to the big picture. Understanding is seeing a snapshot.

"Some of them…" Chip takes a drink of water to ease his dry throat. "…the older souls, have figured out pieces of it. They're not fully in E.G.O.'s clutches, but the majority don't understand how they've been hypnotized by the Elite Global Order's agenda of control."

For the first time in his reign, Lord is speechless.

"That's not all." Chip sits down and clears his throat. "There's a reason I didn't distribute it." His voice drops to a whisper. "I got drunk during dinner and lost it."

"You LOST it?" Lord's lips tighten. "Is this a joke? This is a joke, right?"

"I wish, Father."

"YOU wish?" Lord sighs, with no idea what to say or do. He stares right through Chip. "How did you lose the HOME Law Book, son?"

Chip taps his fingers on the table and grits his teeth.

"HOW DID YOU LOSE IT?"

"I told you. I got drunk at Passover dinner. You know, the Last Supper? When I woke up in the garden, it was gone."

"I told SpirIT turning all that water into wine was a bad idea," Lord mumbles under his breath.

"How I lost it isn't as important as who took it," Chip says matter-of-factly.

Beads of sweat tumble off Lord's forehead. Earth's covered in a warm rain, and for the first time in the history of the planet, water falls to the ground everywhere at once. "Who has it?"

"Cretin," Chip says, not knowing what his father will do next. He remembers hearing people on Earth speak about the "wrath of the Lord," but has never done anything before now to incur it upon himself.

"And…"

13

Lord steels himself.

"...he's fashioned his control of the masses using the tenets of the HOME Law Book to forward his agenda. You've heard of 'the Bible'?"

"Yes."

"Well, without the Law Book, the New Testament would've never been written."

An even more livid Lord trembles, sending a ripple through the cosmos. His reaction adds thunder and lightning and earthquakes to an already-rain-soaked Earth, baffling meteorologists.

"How could I have not known about this?"

"I blocked your access to the Akashic records[10] on this issue."

Lord fumes, just short of exploding. On Earth, an ancient, up-until-now-thought-to-be-dormant volcano erupts.

"I-I-I don't even know what to say," he stutters. "Congratulations. You have rendered Lord of G.O.D. speechless."

"SpirIT guided me."

Chip's tonal inflection alerts SpirIT that he's "coming clean."

"SpirIT instructed you to block me from the Library of Eternity?"

"Well, yes. At first I couldn't believe it myself, but IT told me it was all part of the plan. I was to simply follow IT's direction and keep it between us until further notice." Chip pauses. "Father, since I walk in your footsteps, you know I always listen to SpirIT. And it *was* SpirIT."

---

[10] Also known as the Library of Eternity, the Akashic records log everything that ever happened or will happen.

"You should have come to me sooner, son. Cretin's boss, Lucifer, is a master trickster. She must have masqueaded as SpirIT to trick you into doing E.G.O.'s bidding."

"It was SpirIT who said not to worry, to rest a spell. IT would tell me the right time to tell you," Chip continues. "In my defense, I didn't mind a little break. You never mentioned anything about a crucifixion prior to the last trip to Earth. That dying on the cross thing was brutal! You coulda warned me, Pop. Perhaps if you had protected me…"

"How could you not have distributed Earth's Law Book? And waiting this long to tell me? You know what is at stake! I am so angry with you, I cannot even look at you!"

"I just told you! SpirIT guided me when to tell you."

"I would like to hang you from a cross myself right now," Lord fumes. "And besides, we have been over and over the whole crucifixion thing. It was all part of a plan I had nothing to do with."

"Maybe this is, too, Father. No disrespect."

He just stares at his son. Chip closes his eyes and bows his head, then looks up and flashes a slightly toned-down version of his infectious boyish grin.

"I just finished reading the New Testament, Father, which could also explain the timing of my dream. Cretin used my life as Jesus and the HOME Law Book as a springboard for control, instilling superstitious fears into the hearts of the people and ensnaring them into E.G.O.'s matrix. It should really be spelled B-U-Y-B-U-L-L!" Chip states matter-of-factly.

"Ha!" Lord says flatly. He'd be more amused by the same joke under different circumstances. "No wonder Cretin is winning."

They sit in silence. "SpirIT is in on this?"

"Yes, Father. IT was crystal clear, guaranteeing that upon learning of this event, all Knowledge would be downloaded to you. IT said not to worry."

"Talk about working in mysterious ways," he says, coming to the realization that everything is in divine order. *It has to be.*

SpirIT is delighted with Lord's quick and accurate assessment of the situation, evidenced by beatific music wafting from the SpirIT's grand orchestra. IT telepathically pipes a message to Lord: *Send him back.*

Lord doesn't miss a beat. "You are going back to Earth."

"Back to Earth?"

"You are not surprised, are you?"

"Not really, Father. No. But we need some agreements this time, okay?"

"Agreements?" Lord rolls his eyes. "Are you negotiating with me?"

"Ahh...no..." Chip, realizing he's in no position to make demands, acquiesces.

"Just remember these two things and you will be fine. The first is to be a living demonstration of insight, vision, clarity, kindness, and consideration in your actions and decisions. Do not forget that every moment affects the next, and remember the bigger picture. Consciously keep open not only your mind, but also your heart. Keep learning and refining as the lessons unfold. Stay fluid within your constraints."

Chip dances a little hula, moving his body in the motion of water while his hands make a swimming fish.

Entertained, Lord says, "And two, always eat before you get irritable. Hungry earthlings in any camp make bad decisions."

"The eating part, good advice. But the sad truth is, part one doesn't take into account the condition of E.G.O. and how misguided earthlings are." Chip stops dancing. "Many adhere to their beliefs so strongly that they'll kill for them. Just like when the Romans crucified anyone who didn't sing their tune. Well, I agree what you say is ideal, but I'm not sure it's realistic—coming from practical experience."

"Always remember, son—free will exists to give beings the opportunity to make the better choices!"

"The good news is your intuition was right on," Chip says. "You knew something was wrong. Maybe next time you'll follow it!" He flashes that infectious smile.

Lord gives him a humored "watch it" glance as he signals Gabe and the angels into the room. While they settle, Lord silently calls out to SpirIT, who has been thoroughly enjoying watching the *Lord & Chip Show.*

SpirIT hears the call and ignores it.

In order to imprint The Field, IT offers out loud, "Lord can handle this. I'm going to let him marinate and ruminate on the situation, since this is part of his galactic training. It will allow him to demonstrate the wisdom he has acquired over the centuries. He's got this."

SpirIT directs Lord's call to IT's voice mail. "I can't take your call right now. But I can see you! Hahahaha. *Beep.*"

Then SpirIT summons IT's double bass and plays a bow lightly across the strings.

Lord is instantly tuned. Feeling SpirIT's presence and knowing IT is with him, he raps his fist on the table.

"This meeting is called to Galactic Order. I hope you are ready. We are about to enter hyperspeed."

four

As high tech as they come, Cretin's office is designed to become whatever kind of space he needs it to be. The walls move at the touch of a button and the room transforms into a workspace or a gym or conference room, or becomes suitable for a cocktail soiree. Etcetera.

Cretin, who resembles a large troll doll—albeit with longer legs—is in the gym on the elliptical machine reviewing his keynote speech for TASTE,[11] the biggest event of the century. His speech is the very reason the event's being heralded, since his in-person appearances are rare. Cretin much prefers what he calls "the safety of the shadows"—so much so that some people don't even believe he exists. But with people fighting back against the tightening of their belts and the façade of E.G.O.'s well-manicured spin breaking down, he's being forced to get more involved.

Calling the conference "TASTE" is another example of E.G.O.'s grand deception. It implies the attendees are refined, that they've got discernment and style. Lucifer, Cretin, Gil, Will, and all of E.G.O.'s Powers That Be consider this conference the kickoff to the beginning of the end of any semblance of true freedom among earthlings.

Bring on the smoke. Bring on the mirrors!

Cretin puts the speech down and clicks the remote for the wide-screen television to catch up on the day's

---

[11] E.G.O.'s acronym means Technical Autocratic Slave Tenure Enacted.

news. He watches six stations at once, fully enamored with himself as he witnesses the Elite Global Order's message being continually pumped into the minds of the unsuspecting denizens of planet Earth. They use one distraction after another to keep the majority's attention and outrage exactly where Lucifer and E.G.O. want it.

Suddenly, breaking news appears on every channel, although the story is different on each one: A tsunami warning in California. A surprise eruption of Krakatoa, a volcano thought to be dormant. Earthquakes in Haiti, Mexico, and Argentina. Rain occurring all over the world at the same time...for the first time ever!

"Perhaps we should consider building an ark!" The newscaster guffaws just as lightning hits and takes out the camera.

While meteorologists endlessly contemplate, discuss, and banter with the newscasters about the situation, Cretin knows all these events happening simultaneously can only mean one thing: a huge shake-up in the house of Lord.

Switching the channel, Cretin's jaw drops as he stops in his tracks. *What's this pain-in-my-ass activist Justine Maxim doing getting screen time?* He turns up the volume.

"...global warming," Justine says strongly. "It's time to change our ways. We can do something about this."

"What can viewers do?" Robin Newswoman asks. "What do you suggest?"

"I have never been happier to answer a question," Justine responds. "Combine your words with actions. Demonstrate your disagreement. Pick up the phone,

CALL and COMPLAIN. Tell the oil companies to research, implement, and promote other energy sources.
Then call your government representatives. On a
personal level, use glass instead of plastic, drive less,
walk and bike more... You've got two legs for a reason!
Keep making noise. Demonstrate your unwillingness to
support any company that doesn't do its part."

She holds up a sign. "Here are the top ten oil company CEOs—their home numbers are on my website.
Be sure to call them around dinnertime and tell 'em
your thoughts on the desecration of planet Earth. I've
got good tips for you! Use WhatsApp for the interna-
tional ones—it's free. If you're a little shy or don't know
what to say, visit my website for some scripts and ways
you can personally reduce your dependency on oil and
oil-based products. Do it today, tomorrow, do it the
next."

Justine turns over the sign she's holding, now
advertising her contact information along with some
encouraging words. "The website has tons of information, including actions people can take to fight the good
fight against Monsanto, the erosion of the Constitution,
the TSA. Pick a battle that's dearest to your heart and
fight hard! There are lots of issues for your viewers to
choose from, and they'll be more effective with
passion." She turns toward the camera.

"And be sure to join us at the demonstration outside
the TASTE Conference this weekend. We all have to
give a damn if we don't want to take it anymore. I don't
want to take it anymore, but I can't do this alone..."

Livid at what he's seeing, Cretin flies off the
elliptical and calls Janus Kiro. She's E.G.O.'s Minister

of Department of Spin—externally extolled as Public Affairs.

"Shut her down!" his well-worn face screams into the phone. "How did she get on camera anyway? She's on the 'do not air' list!"

"I can't be everywhere at once," Janus declares. "I don't know, but I'll take care of it."

"Be sure everyone knows who our enemies are and is properly trained with our message as an integral part of their outlook. Get her off the air, sanction the station, and fire the reporter. Remember, Janus, there are others dying to have your job."

"Message received."

"And tighten the reins." Cretin slams the phone down and changes the channels. He dons an all-knowing smile as the week's talking points are broadcast across the networks, touting the benefits of GMOs, justifying wars happening across the globe, reinforcing the importance of government keeping tabs on its citizenry, and encouraging citizens to keep a close eye on their neighbors. Endless celebrity inanities and spottings are covered.

The newscasts are interspersed with EGOtising campaigns for the latest drugs, most delicious beer, and fastest cars. *Ask your doctor, have a Bud, and go for a test drive. Buy. Buy? Buy!*

Without warning, Angel runs into Cretin's office. His assistant, Larry, belatedly announces her arrival over the intercom.

She's truly a vision: tall, blonde, strikingly beautiful. Cretin's wife is also his manager, best friend, confidante, and one of the few who are privy to the whole story of the rise of E.G.O. She's in the inner *inner* circle.

"What are you doing here, beautiful? Aren't you supposed to be promoting the conference somewhere?" Cretin jumps up from behind his desk and gives her a kiss. "Sorry, I'm sweaty..."

"We've got trouble, Crete. Lord found out. He knows!"

"Knows what, Angel?" He walks over to the window and stares out.

"About the Law Book. That Chip never distributed it, and that you stole it. Lord's pissed. And he's got a new, aggressive plan to win souls."

"Go on." Cretin returns to his desk and sits down.

"That's all I've got for now. I came right over."

"Good to know. All that weather had to mean something. I just didn't know what. How did you find out?"

"One of our spies planted at CPR overheard it and sent it down the pipeline. I guess Chip came clean. Something about him being pissed about the crucifixion."

Cretin grins. "Give them a bonus... Anything else?"

"Chip had it on SpirIT's orders to block Lord from certain information. But now he can find out everything."

"We've got to move quickly." Cretin rubs his hands together in mischievous glee. "Things are about to become unrecognizable on Earth."

Angel leans over and gives him a big sensuous kiss as he hits her on the ass. "I've gotta run." She heads toward the door. "Don't want to be late for *Good Morning Americans!*"

"See you for dinner, honey pie," Cretin yells. "Don't forget the kids are joining us."

His troll hair waves as he buzzes Larry after Angel rushes out. "Set up an instant video call with Gil and Zephyr for eleven. And get me some coffee and a protein bar."

"Done," his assistant says. "Anything else?"

"Put EWE's Army[12] on notice that conference attendance is mandatory. Strategies will be revealed and positions assigned. Let them know there are consequences for defiance. And they won't like 'em."

---

[12] E.G.O.'s Workers on Earth.

five

"Ugh, when am I going to get a good night's sleep?" I moan.
I toss and turn after a night of little sleep that follows a series
of sleepless nights. Between the hovering helicopters,
breathing problems, night sweats, and the occasional
earthquake thrown in for shits and giggles, good-night-sleeps
in Los Angeles are few and far between. It's wearing on me.
With my already-precarious enthusiasm for life waning, I
have a little conversation with the highest power I can
imagine.

"There'd better be a point to all this," I growl. "What do
I have to do to get some fucking sleep?"

There's no *please*, no *thank you*—just *do it*.

"What do you need so much admiration for anyway? A
real God could exist without a constant need for gratitude and
recognition."

Perhaps the Holy doesn't care for my approach, since
sleep doesn't come. I readjust my pillow and change my
position, trying one more time to get comfortable. Then I
simply give up. Throwing off the covers, I slowly put my feet
on the floor, rub my head, and face the early morning light.

Too ornery to talk to anyone or to do anything else, I
decide to go for a walk on the beach. Perhaps breathing the
ocean air will help. After all, even winter in Southern
California is known for beautiful colors, a warm sun, and a
tempestuous sea that's often scattered with frolicking
dolphins. *La-de-friggin'-da.*

I drive to the beach, about ten minutes away. Leaving
my shoes in the car, I step barefoot onto the cool damp sand

and amble along the waterline, my feet occasionally kissed by the refreshing, lapping waves.

Tsunami warnings from the earthquake in Japan have been over for a couple of days, but evidence of the threat remains on the beach—sand piled high along the shore for as far as the eye can see.

Even though the sea is more splendid than usual—waves hitting the shore with passion and force, the sky filled with creamy, white clouds, and the temperature a perfect 72 degrees—I still can't shake the soul-deadening malaise.

I scream into the waves, "The beach is beautiful. Big surprise! Who fucking cares?!"

It's almost as if a voice in my head was waiting for the question.

"You care," it says. "If you didn't, you would've killed yourself a long time ago. Think about it, Nanette... You're not a procrastinator."

I laugh out loud. "You do have a point, but it's not off the table, ya know. I can always end it whenever I want."

"You keep telling yourself that."

"I will. It gives me solace."

"Sure, you joke, but underneath it all, you know there are things only you can see that need doing. And you're going to do them. So stop threatening yourself; you can't escape your fate. You are here."

The thought stops me in my tracks. *Give up the idea that I can kill myself at any time?* My safety net? Curious idea. I mean, the voice is correct. If I really want to be dead, why aren't I? I might procrastinate a little, but not for forty years —when I decide to do something, I do it.

For instance, when I was fifteen, I taught myself how to ride a unicycle; practicing every day, falling off and skinning my knees and elbows for two whole weeks until I rode all the way down the driveway and turned the corner with everything intact.

When I was eighteen, I called my biological mother and biological father and initiated meetings.

Years later, I bet the Hasidic comedy group Black Shabbos a thousand bucks I could get them in *People* magazine, even though I didn't know anybody at the rag. Six months later, there they were, on the newsstands.

I come up with ideas and execute them. When I want something to happen, it happens. If I really wanted to be dead, I would be dead right now.

Maybe I don't want to die.

Shit. Now what?

Get ready! Here comes Act II... wafts through my head as I remember the intention I set to lose beliefs and patterns that don't serve me. "I can always end it if I want to" probably isn't the best mantra for manifesting a brighter destiny.

What would it be like to genuinely want to live? I throw my arms up in the air. It's been fun—by all accounts, an interesting life—and yet I wonder how different my approach would be if I were actually in love with this thing called "living." What if I embraced it all?

I bring my arms down, *faklempt*.[13] It's time to jump off the fence of a resistance-filled, half-in, half-out existence into the bright light of day.

Whatever that means.

I recommit to my intention of unraveling the past and vacuuming out the nooks and crannies of my psyche so I can participate in life in a new way. Deeply understanding that no matter what the Tony Robbinses, New Age gurus, therapists, coaches, or healers say, accepting and being comfortable

---

[13] Yiddish, meaning choked up, overwhelmed, or excited. Also spelled *verklempt*.

with being on the planet's going to take more than just simply deciding to do so. Yes, wanting it is a start, but there won't be any turning back from the deep inner work no one can do for me.

I race to the shoreline and splash water on my face. Feeling refreshed from the slap of cold sea, I know what I must do: completely embody this new understanding: I. Want. To. Live. The intention I set for Act II is already unraveling me.

***

The beach, with all its elements and tonal sound offerings, is the perfect sanctuary to contemplate this new thinking. While walking along, breathing in the sea air and doing my best to melt into the moment, down the shore I notice someone sitting on a beach chair in the surf. The closer I get, I'm amazed to realize it's someone I know. And, unfortunately, if it's not the last person I want to see right then, it's close. I consider turning around but think better of allowing myself to be thrown off course by something so insignificant. I boldly carry on.

"Bella! What are you doing here?"

"Soaking my feet in the healing waters of the Pacific." She flashes me a big grin—way too cheery for any time of day. "Good to see you, Nanette! What are you doing here so early?"

"Clearing my head." I pick up a flat rock and attempt to skip it across the water. "And you? Are you really using the ocean as a footbath? Yep, I guess you are."

I remember that I don't want to engage in conversation, but it might be too late as Bella holds up one foot and points to a bandage. "Oh. I hope that heals. Okay, see you," I say, almost making a clean getaway.

"Hey, have you read *The Secret*?"[14]

My stomach's never strong enough for this conversation with anybody at any time.

"It's all about the power of your mind, and how what you believe creates the world—"

"It should have been kept secret," I reply. "And besides, your beliefs create YOUR world, not THE world. Universal laws don't bend to your beliefs."

"Well, it's not really working." Bella's obviously lost in a world of her own making. "But I think I'm doing it wrong."

Even though the mention of *The Secret* frosts the top of my New Age pet peeve cake—followed by the indiscriminate use of the words "abundance" and "co-create"—I take the bait and reply, "Bella, the problems with affirmations are twofold. First, you cannot get the prize without doing the work, and second, as Pema Chodron says, 'Affirmations are like screaming that you're okay in order to overcome this whisper that you're not.'"[15]

Bella shouts to the ethers, "I deserve love…I deserve LOVE…" and swishes her feet in the water.

As she chants away, the voice in my head points out the unfathomable chance of Bella appearing on my walk.

"Perhaps there's something in this for you," the voice teases. "Perhaps she carries a piece of the puzzle. Could be synchronistic. Get curious!"

---

[14] Best-selling self-help book by Rhonda Byrne, Atria Books/Beyond Words Publishing, 2006.

[15] Pema Chödrön, Start Where You Are: A Guide to Compassionate Living, Shambhala, 2001.

"Get curious" is always good advice to listen to. "Bella!" An effort's required to pull her out of her affirmative flow. "Bella!"

She shakes her head as if coming out of a trance.

"Let me ask you something, Bella... Do you believe life is a gift?"

The sound of her name the third time finally claims her attention.

"Of course life's a gift." She starts chanting, "Life's a gift I open every day..."

It's all I can do not to projectile vomit into the healing waters of the Pacific.

"I deserve to be loved!" Bella decrees. "Life's a gift!" She gets up and twirls around on her good foot.

Quickly discounting my newfound lease on life, I continue. "Bella... What if I told you that no matter how much I try, I just don't see it? Being in a body feels like a prison to me. All I've ever wanted is out."

"You are kinda intense," she says. "Still cooking for the monks?"

"Priests. I'm surprised you remember."

"Jesuits, right?"

"Yup. Five years now."

"Maybe you're trying too hard!" Bella spins around, falls down, and lays on the beach staring into space. "Consider viewing life from a different angle," she offers. "Relax a little. Accept things." She rolls over, jumps up, takes a warrior's pose, and looks at me with a glint in her eye.

Even though it's coming from someone who's soaking her feet in the Pacific Ocean while chanting affirmations and contemplating *The Secret,* I'm moved by the simplicity and profundity of her response. The entertainment factor doesn't hurt either.

"Hmm. Stop trying so hard. Accept things. Interesting," I say. "Teaching what you need to learn, Bella?" We laugh.

"Hope to see you soon, Nanette. I'll pray for you."

***

I continue along the beach, doing my best to pay attention to my breathing instead of my mind's chatter, which is now trying very hard to stop trying so hard.

Some of the occasionally profound, sometimes inane tools I've gathered over the years race into my mind: various methods of centering and balancing and connecting. They span from my obnoxious New Age phase to my phase of exploring the world of quantum physics. Lately, I've been morphing into an indigenous culture, nature-based wisdom understanding.

I flash on learning how to connect with the Akashic records—a "library in the sky" said to contain the knowledge of all human experience—and decide to give it a shot.

I sit down and quiet myself, and after reciting the secret Entrance Prayer I learned in a weekend workshop, I address the records aloud.

"How can I take the concept of 'trying' out of my vocabulary? I mean, it works when one's talking about food: 'Try this!' But not when it comes to taking actions.

"Try to pick up this shell." I pick up a shell. "Either I pick it up or I don't. There is no 'try.' "

"Ahh, good question," I hear in my heart's ear.

And how about when someone says, "I'll try to be there." Usually it's just an indirect way of saying "I'm not coming." There are exceptions, but…

"Nanette, you're one of our truth-seeking gems. You bring us great joy! We will try to make this clear for you!"

Ha! You make me smile, too!

"You can take the word 'try' out of your vocabulary, but you must also take 'the try' out of your actions. Acceptance is the place from which you can create change."

Take trying out of my actions? What does that have to do with acceptance? Please say more.

"May we be direct?"

"Uh, okay." The records usually don't ask for permission before answering.

"Whenever you want to be a part of something, or whenever you want to impress someone, or you want to show what you've got, you easily lose yourself and give yourself away. You try to get attention in circuitous ways, all the while undervaluing yourself. We have a name for this. It's called 'dancing for acceptance.' "

"Dancing…"

"…for acceptance," the records reiterate. "What do you think it means?"

"Well, I get an image in my head of a person with a cane and a top hat tap-dancing before someone in an effort to gain their admiration. The dancer's feet keep going faster and faster, exhausting themselves while trying to be seen."

"Yes, and…"

"Instead of stopping the dance and realizing their need for recognition, their feet just keep going. Ahh, this is hitting home."

"Can you remember a time when you've chosen this style of communication?"

Oh, boy—I sure can. Memories of feeling disappointment and frustration enter my field of awareness.

"We're all ears," the records say.

"All kinds of memories are flowing in," I say into the air. "Instances where I perceived something incorrectly and started interacting with the perception instead of the person before me; occasions when I got embarrassed, and instead of just speaking up, became more agreeable than I wanted to be. The times when I wanted certain people to see how smart I am, and how much I could help them, so I worked for free, hoping to be recognized, when these people would never hire me—or anybody—for whatever reason. Yes. This is perfect. Just what I needed to hear. Thank you."

The wisdom of these words pierce a veil I've worn for a long time: low self-esteem wrapped in entitlement. Filled with the times in the past I've done things against my better judgment because I wanted to be liked or accepted, I'm sick to my stomach.

How often have I danced for people, trying to get their attention? I should have just stood strong in the wisdom, knowledge, and pool of experience I've accumulated over the years, presenting myself as a valuable commodity. I've spoken up on little matters so frequently! But how do I handle it when something big is at stake?

Stop trying. Stop dancing.

Step in authentically. Bring forth my gifts and present them, all the while respecting myself as much as I respect others.

Whew! What a great time for this lesson.

I hear my name being called and am instantly back on the beach. Even though it's a dear friend, I would prefer not being bothered.

"Nanette! What are you doing here?" Justine Maxim asks. "I was going to call you later."

"It's not even seven thirty in the morning and I've already run into two people I know. So much for a quiet walk!"

"Good to see you, too," Justine replies sarcastically.

"Sorry—I'm in the middle of something and hearing my name being called jarred me."

"I just got back from DC. The fucking TSA! It should be an acronym for Traveler's Sexual Assault. Did you catch me on the news?"

"Uh, no... You've had way too much coffee." In an effort to practice taking care of myself, I say, "I'm going to keep walking. Can't talk now..."

"You okay?" Justine asks.

"Yeah. I'm just in the middle of something."

"Call me later," she says as she jogs off in the other direction.

Alone on the beach, I find myself exhilarated and terrified all at the same time. My life is changing and I have to let it change me. I'm getting what I asked for! I've always said that once you know something, you cannot not know it, which is the double-edged razor of knowing anything. Knowing things...

Shit. Today's Wednesday. Traffic court.

I've got less than two hours to get there to fight a ticket for taking an illegal left turn. I hoof it back to the car, head home, and change into more appropriate attire. This is one fight I'm looking forward to.

Even though my friends have repeatedly called me crazy, I'm convinced that if I go into court and simply tell the judge the truth of what happened, I'll get off.

"Go to traffic school," has become their refrain. "It's better than points[16] and higher insurance."

---

[16] "Points" refer to a system in which a driver's licensing authority issues cumulative demerits, or points, to drivers for road traffic offenses. Points are typically applied after an offense and cancelled after a defined period. If the total number of points exceeds a specified limit, the offender may not be allowed to drive for a time. Fines and other penalties may be applied additionally. California is one state that uses a point system.

But I know differently.

***

Racing, I arrive in the courtroom just in time. The room is called to order and the judge spells out all the ways defendants can plead: "And if you plead 'not guilty," she explains, "you'll be given a later court date to allow the officer an opportunity to show up and plead his case. If he doesn't make it, your case will be dismissed."

For a quick instant, I consider changing my tactics and pleading not guilty, but right then I hear my name being called. So I pass through a little gate and stand before the judge.

"Nanette Kenyon, how do you plead?"

"Can I plead guilty with an explanation?"

"Yes," she says. "Please continue." I imagine her thinking to herself, *I can't wait to hear this one.*

"Thank you, Your Honor. I took a new route to the novitiate, where I work as a cook for Jesuit priests." I figure any reference to divinity can't hurt. "I stopped to take a left turn. Cars behind me were honking. I saw the officer sitting there, but I just didn't see the sign. I wouldn't have turned if I saw it. I spaced out."

The judge looks me square in the eye and says, "You spaced out?"

"Yes, I spaced out."

"You spaced out?" she asks again.

I nod my head yes.

The gavel hits the podium and the judge declares, "Case dismissed."

I grin from cheek to cheek.

"Please step up to the bench, Ms. Kenyon," requests the judge. I obey. She whispers, "I've been waiting twenty years for someone to tell me the unembellished truth. You just made my day."

"Thank you! This might be the first time the truth literally set me free!"

The judge appreciates my humor.

Something inside told me to fight that ticket with what actually happened, and I listened.

***

Nanette's experience doesn't go unnoticed by Lord, who marvels at how well she followed The Field Prompts[17] on this one.

She didn't know it at the time, but the court case was a demonstration of her willingness to follow the prompts. She passed the test. *Consciousness Competency Testing*, Lord calls it. It's one of his favorite parts of the job.

---

[17] Field Prompts: Whispers or shouts from The Field that offer guidance, if received and followed. They can come from anywhere—people, animals, birds, nature, license plates, billboards—whatever means work for the moment.

six

Looking sharp in his Armani suit, Larry brings Cretin his coffee and snack. Three weeks on the job and he's more on top of things than Cretin's last assistant was after ten years. Larry's no dummy and is excellent at getting what he wants—behind-the-scenes information about how the whole E.G.O. empire *really* works. All the while, he presents himself in an extremely impressive package.

Larry's wealthy family has left him so well off that he doesn't have to work—or do anything, really. He's not so much political as he is interested in patterns, trends, and putting together the puzzle pieces of a bigger picture.

Back at his desk, Larry's first call about the meeting is to Gil Gamesh, CEO of Time/Space Corporation. The best way to describe Time/Space's reach is that if you believe everything in this universe really comes from one infinite source—despite its separate appearances—that source is Time/Space Corp. Little do people know that among the major corporations, there's no competition. It's all an illusion designed to keep the masses busy with this and that. All roads eventually lead back to Time/Space.

Cretin trusts Gil with his life, and for good reason, Gil credits Cretin with saving his soul during a time he doesn't like to talk about. He's forever indebted to him.

"What's on the agenda, Larry?" Gil asks. "What's the urgency?"

"I'm not sure. Angel came and went and he told me to clear his schedule and set up this meeting. Something big."

"Who else is on the call?"

"Just you, Cretin, and Zephyr."

"Okay. See you then."

Larry hangs up and dials again. "Good morning, Zephyr," he says. "Cretin's called a video conference at eleven."

"Not a good time for me. We're just getting the main stage hoisted, screens set up, and teleports wired. My focus needs to be here.

"Not there, THERE!" he shouts, illuminating his point.

Zephyr dislikes complying with these kinds of requests even though Cretin's a high-ranking E.G.O. official. Because he was raised in complete under-standing of the laws of the Galactic Order and how they shape the laws and structures of the Elite Order's global control, Zephyr's heart has always been more with G.O.D. than with E.G.O. But due to family oblige-tions, this is where he finds himself. His rank, lower than Cretin or Gil, causes immense anxiety within his extremely attractive 5'10" frame. You see, he has more heart and intelligence in his pinky than both of them put together.

Zephyr has accidentally revealed his predilection toward G.O.D. in the past, placing him in an awkward position with his upper-crust family. Now he's on probation; being the executive producer of the TASTE Conference is his final chance to prove to his parents his unflinching support for E.G.O. and its tenets. If he doesn't, he'll be disowned, disinherited, done—

completely removed from all family duties, protections, and financial support.

He's not sure the wages are worth what he calls "gut-wrenching, soul-crushing, mind-numbing" chores and commitments, and the silent promises inherent in operating within the family, but the thought of not having that safety net feels equally, if not more, scary. Cretin keeps giving orders that override Zephyr's intuitive leanings, and he certainly doesn't appreciate being called "insubordinate" when he doesn't readily jump to Cretin's demands.

Larry, acutely aware of the chasm between them, is always ready for resistance when summoning the one he affectionately calls, "his Zephyrness."

"I recommend working out your attendance. There's important news."

"I'll be there," Zephyr concedes. "But I don't know what could be more important than the proper functioning of main stage at the conference."

"Only one way to find out. Hope you make the right decision." Larry hangs up.

***

The eleven a.m. videoconference begins on time. Cretin gets right to business.

"The matrix on Earth has changed. The combination of Lord learning what happened and the masses questioning our influences can only lead to us losing control. Once the truth's out—"

"The timing on this couldn't be better." Zephyr is secretly *kvelling*[18] in the possibility of G.O.D.'s rise in

---

[18] Derived from the Yiddish, *kveln*, meaning "to be delighted" or "so excited about something."

popularity. Still, he feigns allegiance. "We've got the perfect platform to spin the future—the conference!"

Ignoring him, Cretin continues. "These over-standings have never before been openly available to earthlings. Those who take them to heart will have the ability to see through our story and connect to the bigger picture at will. They'll disengage once they realize the innate powers and built-in laws they have on their side."

As he speaks, the gravity of the situation dawns on Gil and Zephyr. Cretin stomps around his office, moving in and out of the video.

"Gil, start the draft. And train those inductees immediately."

"We've got some brilliant control programs launch-ing," Zephyr continues, undaunted. "The full potential of the TSA has yet to be exploited, the recession's just rolling out, and the effects of eating GMOs for the last twenty years are only now beginning to wreak havoc on the health of the general population. There's nothing to worry about!"

Zephyr doesn't notice Gil's eye-rolling in response to his weak and tired ideas. "We have so many tricks up our sleeves that have yet to be revealed. Right?"

Cretin, who doesn't have time for this shit, shakes his head. "O Busy One, you have no idea what you're talking about."

Gil, annoyed by the optimistic twit on every level, wants to smash Zephyr like a bug. "Now that Lord realizes what's going on down here, nothing will remain the same. Don't kid yourself, Zephy. Some new frilly programs and slogans aren't going to tie this one into a pretty bow."

"My name is Zephyr."

"Enough," their boss commands. "Never mistake motion for action. We will not move too quickly, or without a plan."

Zephyr looks directly at his colleague and scratches an itch in the corner of his eye with his middle finger.

Cretin continues pacing, coming in and out of camera range. "We'll only move smart. Yes, the bar was just raised. With Lord aggressively waking people up to the range of their innate powers, souls are going to be positively unmanageable, *and* they're going to learn of their inalienable right to demonstrate their unconditional autonomy. We simply cannot allow them to have the leisure time they need to learn the workings and the power of The Field." He closes his eyes and contemplates the situation.

"We've been preparing for this moment all along. People are busy by design, you know," Gil points out.

"Right. We'll use the systems already in place. Inundate everyone! More politics, more paperwork, more rules under the guise of security, more taxes, more issues, more wars, less time, more prescription drugs—"

"—more celebrity distractions!" Zephyr shouts.

Cretin continues sternly. "We must vigorously promote our God. It's crucial that we keep the G.O.D./God teachings confusing.

"Continue feeding the public opposing viewpoints of every story. They'll squabble among themselves on unimportant issues—engaged and full of fear, with no time to pay attention to anything except keeping their heads above water. As the belts keep tightening, people will struggle against the system rather than fight for a life they cannot even imagine exists because they're just too damn tired. They'll have no choice but to ignore G.O.D.'s teachings and The Field.

"Raise prices on EVERYTHING!" the troll commands. "Keep the general public as stressed as possible. Gil, see to it that every stoplight is lengthened for at least an additional minute..."

Gil brightens at the request. Anxiousness-raising is one of his favorite activities.

"...and anything else you can think of."

Zephyr drifts off for a second, daydreaming about Lord and G.O.D. prevailing over the planet with stewardship. He'd rather live free in a garden than be an authority in a dictatorship. In his mind, even if you're the warden, you're still in prison.

"Is that all for now?" Zephyr asks tersely. "I have work to do."

"Dismissed," Cretin says. "But don't you forget, Busy One, that your position in this organization is under review."

Zephyr disconnects. Gil hangs on while Cretin buzzes Larry. So far, he's beyond satisfied with his new assistant's service—appreciating his forthrightness, sass, and the manner in which he executes his tasks. Since Larry has nothing to lose, he unknowingly exudes a confidence and calm demeanor that intrigues Cretin. His degrees in sociology, philosophy, and psychiatry *almost* impress him.

On his side of the video feed, Gil cringes as Cretin shouts at Larry, "Set up a daylong Cremation of Care[19] ceremony at The Grove for Friday beginning at six a.m. sharp. Let the Board members know plans have changed; we'll be staying the weekend and broadcasting our presence at TASTE from there. Make sure women Board members know the 'men only' rule is suspended for the weekend. Attendance is mandatory.

"And book the Oracle, Lakshmi, to arrive at exactly nine a.m. Let her know we need a directional reading. Now, patch in *Good Morning Americans* for Gil and me. Angel should be on any minute."

GMA comes through just in time for them to catch the tail end of his wife's appearance.

"So you see..." Angel's voice floats out from their screens. "...if your house is being foreclosed upon, it's really God's way of telling you it's time for you to go somewhere else. He 'moves' in mysterious ways, you know." She indicates quote marks with her fingers and laughs at her own pun, and then emphasizes sincerity. "Sometimes a kick in the ass is a step forward."

Almost speechless but always a professional, Robin Newswoman takes it all in. "Hmm. Interesting ideas."

"Anything else you want to talk about, dear?"

---

[19] The "Cremation of Care" is an annual theatrical production written, produced, and performed by and for members of the Bohemian Club. It is staged at the Bohemian Grove near Monte Rio, California, at a small artificial lake amid a private, old-growth grove of Redwood trees. The dramatic performance is presented on the first night of the annual encampment as an allegorical banishing of worldly cares for the club members, and "to present symbolically the salvation of the trees by the club," but the secretive nature of the Bohemians, and the political power of some of its members, has attracted notice from conspiracy theorists. Wikipedia.

"What do you make of all this crazy weather?" Robin asks. "Do you think these are the 'end times' as people say?"

Angel nonchalantly throws her head back. For impact, she looks directly into the camera. "These are beginning times. These are the times we've been waiting for! The weather? A dramatic welcome to a new, exciting era—nothing more. Enjoy the rain! Water brings growth. Don't let it stop us from seeing you at the conference this weekend!"

"Boy, she's good," Gil acknowledges as text promoting the conference crawls across the bottom of the screen.

"That's why we call her the Queen of Masked Transparency." Cretin puffs out his chest. "That's why I love her."

"We oughta make her the face of Time/Space." Gil stares off into the distance, lost in thought. "Yeah, nothing like using a beautiful blond named Angel as a distraction from the coming societal reconstruction."

seven

Lord, ready to begin, shoots a multicolored spark into the air, commanding the space as only he can.

"The facts are in. Chip never distributed the HOME Law Book. Cretin got his hands on the only copy available on Earth and...'took creative license.' He used it to fashion the Elite Global Order's reign over earthlings and created an all-knowing, all-seeing, all punishing entity called 'God.' It is pretty brilliant, actually—creating an invisible warden to do your bidding."

"One with the same name as The Field,"[20] Gabe says. "No wonder people are so confused."

Lord paces. "Turns out Cretin and E.G.O. have fabricated a universally accepted belief system and engaged just about every born soul into a conveyor-belt existence—a one-way life path from birth to death. The beliefs he promotes intermittently incorporate wisdom from the HOME Law Book, but incorrectly."

He stops and stands still with his brow furrowing as his overstanding increases. "They are using this info to gain control instead of instill natural order, and because these stories and illusions are accepted as *the way it is*, truth must walk down a long reception line before even being considered."

"Seems pretty well-thought-out," Chip comments.

---

[20] G.O.D. is the name of the container—aka The Field. E.G.O. calls their made-up, all-seeing entity *God* also. Once people discover the truth, it can be still difficult to determine which is which without practice.

"So E.G.O.—with its invisible God—has been keeping the masses in line? If I may be so bold, Lord," Gabe asks, "how did this little tidbit slip by you?"

"Trust me, it was by design." Lord winks toward SpirIT. "The good news is our plan is set to roll out exponentially, starting with tapping Team AWE—our Awakened Weavers on Earth. Each team member was born with an innate trigger: a sound, an image, an interaction, a specific word, an event. Throughout their lives, they have experienced bits and pieces of mystical entrainments. When activated, they will join together to awaken earthlings to the majesty of demonstrating Universal law and becoming human beings."

Chip, Gabe, and the other angels—Colopatiron, Michael, Nathaniel, and Paschar—settle into their chairs with their ears pricked, waiting to hear the story of their future.

Lord continues. "So, the plan. Chip is going back to Earth to (a) hire, (b) groom, and (c) work with our new publicist, Nanette Kenyon. Yes. That is right." He nods at the surprised faces. "We are hiring a publicist."

"A publicist? ... Really?" Gabriel takes in the idea. "Fantastic!"

"Her job is four-fold, as follows: One, to help distribute the Law Book. Two, to activate and anchor Team AWE. Three, to explain the true nature of G.O.D., including promoting and demonstrating demonstration and the laws of the Earth game. Four, to head CPR ~ EARTH."[21]

"Are we going to Earth too?" Paschar perks up. "That would be most exciting!"

"Perhaps. You will be where you are needed when you are needed there. That is all you need to know for now."

---

[21] Center Presenting Reality ~ Earth Branch.

"I haven't been to Earth in centuries!" Colopatiron says to Paschar. "I telecommute."

They all laugh. Angel humor.

"Michael is in charge," Lord continues. "Any questions or problems? Go to him. He is the instrument of communication from Gabe and me to you, and vice versa."

They all nod in acknowledgement.

"Tell us about her, please...this Nanette. Has she been granted advanced seeing?"

"Not full access quite yet; she only experiences advanced seeing here and there. She is starting to recognize and acknowledge the experience, but she does not really know what it is yet. SpirIT tells me we have been grooming her for this position over lifetimes..."

He looks at Chip. "Your job of prepping her for her role in the Galactic Order is going to be a challenging one. As aware and reverent as she is, she is equally feisty and irreverent. She does not like to be told what to do. You will see. She has been 'softened' over the past decade or so, but still has some rough edges. Do not worry, though, son. You have the support of Gabriel, the angels, me, The Field...and, of course, you are YOU!!! And you are powerful."

Lord tosses a ball of energy into the air. It explodes into a beautiful mountain scene with a dark plume of smoke rising out of the northwest corner.

"Aw, shucks." Chip shrugs and blushes.

"Notice the direction of the smoke. That's not by chance."

"Ahh, yes. The northwest is all about liberation. Fitting." Chip tries to step into Lord's projection as the image vanishes.

"One more thing." Lord's voice deepens. "You have seven days."

"Seven days! To convince her to be the publicist for G.O.D. and do all that? Surely you jest…"

"What exactly is our strategy?" Gabriel jumps in. "Do we have a marketing plan? And is it seven Earth days or seven galactic days?"

"I am glad you asked that question." Lord turns the room into a small planetarium with the night sky projected on the ceiling. "First, galactic days…"

Chip lets out a deep sigh of relief. His shoulders drop as tension visibly leaves his body.

"Don't get too comfortable. It's seven galactic days to get her on board and consciously demonstrating awareness. Could be a tall order. During that time, you can go over the Law Book together and she can embody it."

"A brushup couldn't hurt me, either," Chip admits.

"I am glad you agree. It has certainly been a while for you. And Nanette, well… Let us just say she was born with a voracious appetite for the truth." He fondles his beard. "And she is not stopping until she exemplifies it, exudes it, epitomizes it—"

"Sounds like a real firecracker," Chip breaks in.

"She has embraced many of the laws from her own explorations on Earth," Lord continues, "but does not have the bandwidth to consistently broadcast the experience. She is still in need of some societal de-programming, yet she is getting pretty good at catching herself when she is entangled in and operating from implanted belief systems. She just demonstrated brilliant listening and it got her out of a traffic ticket! You will have fun with her."

He swivels around, facing Gabe.

"You asked if we have a marketing plan. We do, and this new, innovative way to move forward is something to get excited about. The plan is fluid; it flexes as information, criteria, and circumstances change. Our top priorities are to show earthlings the truth about what the Galactic Order of Demonstration is and who this God is not. It will not be an easy task; their belief systems will be shaken up beyond their wildest dreams.

"We will also focus on waking up Team AWE. Each awakened weaver exponentially expands our reach. The ripple effect is really quite beautiful, and it is one of our greatest offerings. As more and more AWEs are moved into action, a tipping point will be reached." Lord directs his attention to Chip.

"And we will distribute the Law Book."

"But of course, Your Honor!" Chip bows before him half-mockingly.

Lord wraps up his initial directions. "Finally, we are opening CPR ~ EARTH, so Chip—and anyone else who needs to—has a place to meet and be nourished."

"A place to hang our wings!" Michael extends and flaps his ever so gently, careful not to create too much of a breeze.

"Finally," Lord continues, "Gabe, you will be taking a trip to Earth to install a version of the Map in the new offices and train the staff in its workings."

Gabe sits a little taller. The truly ingenious Sheet of the World, also referred to as "the Map," secured his position as Chief Programmer in the Galactic Order for eternity. Automatically upgraded with the absolute latest in technological advances, the Map tracks what camp any earthling is in, where they're located, what they're doing, and how well they're demonstrating knowing. It shows when they uncover the "Clue of the Obstacle,"[22] and so much more. The data it reveals can keep one entertained for hours.

"Clue of the Obstacle?" Michael asks. Lord nods toward his programmer, indicating he should answer.

"It's really ingenious!" Gabe gushes. "Every seeming problem is an answer to a request. Once you find out where they meet, you've found the clue—to understanding, to over-standing...to resolution! It's so important to remember what you ASKed for in relation to what is happening."

"We want the rollout to be smooth, elegant, and timely," Lord continues. "Cretin and the Elite Global Order will not tolerate losing souls without raising the stakes. We need to utilize our deepest strengths, and we *will* prevail. LOVE has to, right?"

"Right!" Fists rise in solidarity.

"And mechanics. LOVE and the mechanics of the container," Lord clarifies.

"Say more," Gabe asks, "for the benefit of the team?"

"Earth is a mechanical field. It operates in the same manner for everyone, if you know how to work it. E.G.O. has people believing that in order to receive 'blessings,' you have to take Jesus Christ as your personal savior. The truth is that all you have to do is exist and the power is yours... There will be more on this later. Maybe one night over martinis."

Gabe shudders with delight. The group knows that in his mind, there's nothing better than a nice, dry martini with Lord.

"I will say this: At the moment, it seems Cretin and E.G.O. have the upper hand—*seems* being the key word. They have been responsible for piping in the 'life in general'

---

[22] The thing you think is in the way of your path *is* your path, and is usually directly in response to something you asked for, sometimes indirectly. This appreciation is the Clue of the Obstacle.

information stream for centuries, but fear not, dear ones. Truth will prevail. And truth is so much more discerning than any fabricated story.

"Chip, go prepare for your trip. Gabriel, program the Map to receive the new marketing plan data. Angels, carry on and wait for direction. Anything else?"

Lord scans The Field, satisfied. "Meeting adjourned."

***

Chip dances around to Carole King's "I Feel The Earth Move" as he gets ready for his journey. He summons the Akashic records to provide him with a present-day translation of the Law Book in English, the language of the United States of America, where he will begin teaching.

As he fills his knapsack with seeds, teas, comfortable clothing, and sandals, he remembers some of his favorite events and places from the last time he visited. He looks forward to the aroma of pine needles and the feeling of sunshine; the pastel layering of a beautiful sunset; one-on-one interaction with Earth folk; and last, but first—a taste of Earth coffee.

He's heard so much about it over the years, and no other Galactic Order has it.

***

Lord wakes up from a much-needed nap, then immediately summons Chip, Gabe, and Michael using indranet, The Field's built-in communication system. The network is available to every living thing, always, but earthlings stopped listening—or being able to hear—long ago amid all the noise and static generated by E.G.O.

The team promptly turns up in Lord's presence. He reveals a few final details.

"All your questions will be answered on a need-to-know basis. You will know everything you need to know and have everything you need to have at the moment you need to know it and the moment you have to have it. From now on, you are required to live and act in as much faith and trust as we ask from earthlings and Team AWE. Field Prompts are always there…pay attention to receive them! But remember to acknowledge The Field for the prompt. A wink or a nod is enough. It's not about The Field needing gratitude—simply put, it is important for you to let on that you recognize the interplay. When you are InFlow,[23] everything is before you. Oh, a parting gift…"

He hands each of them a personal medicine bag filled with amulets, talismans, herbal teas, and assorted goodies.

"As luck would have it, you will also be hearing from me," Lord says cheerily. "Those are guaranteed to be broadcasts you do not want to miss."

"Can't wait!" Chip says. "I'm ready for this adventure. Getting Earth back on track to being the paradise planet it was meant to be—the educational playground of the universe, the precious vacation spot from the overcrowded collective—is a noble effort. Yep. I'm ready."

"Okay, get moving." Lord hugs Chip, patting him on the back. "It is time to witness InFlow in action."

Chip holds his father tight. They kiss each other on both cheeks. "If there's nothing more, I'm outta here."

With that, Chip—with his special purpose of securing G.O.D.'s new publicist—disappears and lands outside a courtroom in downtown Los Angeles, just as…

---

[23] The term used to describe following G.O.D.'s universal laws of demonstration, or operating in alignment with The Field.

PART TWO

eight

I skip out of the courthouse, hungry and feeling great. I knew I would win—like a message from the universe. This was some sort of a test, and I passed. *I just have no idea what I'm being tested for!*

The question now is, where do I go to celebrate my victory?

I begin dialing my best friend to tell her the fantastic news. A casually dressed yet beautiful man in front of me is too distracting, though, to continue. His gentle yet crisp features, combined with his blue eyes and brown hair, have me frozen, locked in an embarrassing stare.

"Good day!" He approaches and extends his palm. "I'm Chip."

"Uh-hello." I snap out of it and back up as he moves toward me. "Can I help you with something?"

"Nanette Kenyon? I'm looking for you."

"Huh? Looking for me for what?"

"How about if we discuss that over breakfast?"

"Who are you?"

"Come on, I'm starving. Have breakfast with me and I'll tell you everything. Don't worry. I'm as safe as is cosmically possible." A bluebird lands on his shoulder. The man winks at the bird as I look him up and down. The bird takes off.

"What do you want?" Besides being breathtaking, his face is beaming.

"It'll be better over food," Chip says.

Sometimes a girl just has to say yes. "Okay, I'll join you. I've been asking lately for the opportunity to meet some

interesting men who haven't taken vows. You haven't, have
you?"

Chip hesitates. "Uh, no. No vows." He holds up his left
hand and wiggles his bare ring finger.

"Hmm. God seems to be delivering today."

"You have no idea."

The man sounds as if he has the market cornered on God
experiences. "Try me." I spread open my arms and look up as
if I'm receiving energy from above, then back to Chip.
"Well, as long as it's a public place. I can always get up and
leave if you get too weird."

"True."

So off we go toward The Downtown Diner—a sweet
little spot with delicious coffee and good food. "Breakfast's
on me," Chip offers.

"Yes, it is," I assure him.

We're seated right away with menus and water.
"Coffee," Chip and I say in unison to our hostess. As she
departs, I immediately bombard him with questions.

"Do you mind?" Chip raises his eyebrow. "Can we get
some food before we start the interrogation?"

The waitress appears and takes our order. We both get
frittatas with crispy bacon, fruit, and toast.

Chip examines the tabletop, touching the salt and pepper
shakers, jelly packets, and a syrup container. "The good news
is that all of your questions will be answered. Maybe not in
the order you ask them... And for certain not all at once."

"Oookay." I consciously stop my leg from nervously
bouncing, something that rarely happens anymore.

"The first question I'll answer is, 'What do I want?'
Well, it's not actually what I want... It's what my father
wants."

"Who's your father? Do I know him?"

"Well, you'll have to tell me if you know him, but he certainly knows you."

"What's his name?"

The waitress delivers the coffee. I take a sip.

"First, let me tell you about the job."

I choke on my coffee. "Job? What job?"

"You've had some great successes with publicity and live event production, haven't you?" Chip asks as he points to a spot on his chin and hands me a napkin, not missing a beat.

"Publicity? Sure… But I quit doing that a while ago— the same time I quit managing the unmanageable. Comedians, I mean."

"Why did you quit?" He takes a sip of coffee. A look of eternal bliss floats across his sweet face just as the food arrives. "These potatoes look delicious!" Chip takes a bite. His moan with pleasure tells me he's a foodie at heart. "Coffee is everything it's cracked up to be."

With a knowing nod, I go on. "It was time. I'd had enough." I dig into my frittata. "Well, the truth is, I gave it up because of the sauce."

"The sauce? You've got a drinking problem?" The man looks positively flabbergasted. "No one mentioned that to me," he mutters.

"Nope. Balsamic Butter Sauce. I made some one day and my taste buds flew open. In that instant, I knew I loved cooking more than dealing with neurotic performers."

"You'll have to make that for me some time." I nonchalantly nod. "I'm not joking," Chip says.

"Nothing has ever equaled the sense of contentment I feel when I hear the symphony of silence accompanying the first bite of a good meal." I drift off into the memory of the best croissant I ever had…crispy, flaky, perfect texture…ahh.

Chip folds his palms and raises his eyebrows. "Let's see—publicity."

I snap out of it. "And food doesn't lie. It cannot pretend to be good when it isn't."

"I'm thinking you're going to want to take it up again."

"Doubtful, but I'm listening."

"I'm here to hire you to do publicity for a noteworthy client. And he won't take no for an answer, so—"

"Won't take no for an answer?" The hair on the back of my neck rises and my demeanor changes. "We'll see about that. As I mentioned, I quit doing PR."

***

Chip, noticing her change in tone, connects with CPR. Lord feels a little bothered by the call, as this is really Earth Communications 101, the most basic of understandings. He forwards the call to Gabe, but listens in.

"Chip," Gabe says, "wake up! You can't tell someone who doesn't want anyone telling her what to do that she has no choice. Demonstrate your knowing and pay attention!"

"Pay attention!" Lord says, echoing Gabe. "Remember, attention is the price of wisdom. The phrase 'PAY attention' is not random."

"Oh, yes. I remember." Chip aligns. "Attention is tuition for awareness. It's all coming back to me."

Chip is InFlow and brings his focus back to Nanette and her words.

***

"Listen here, Chipster. You didn't do your vetting. Nanette Kenyon always has a choice." My leg starts motoring again as I take a bite of toast. I continue to talk while chewing, at the same time realizing that eating right then probably wasn't the best idea. "Besides, getting me back into PR would cost a pretty penny—probably more than your daddy wants to spend." I consciously stop my leg.

"What I meant to say is, once you find out about the length, width, and depth of this project, you won't want to say no, not that you couldn't. I apologize for ruffling your feathers. Didn't mean to."

After swallowing my food, I take a drink of coffee. Now I'm even more intrigued. A man who can tell he pissed me off and immediately acknowledges and handles it. This is rare and interesting. *Is there a name for this species?*

"Oh no—I did my homework. I know all about you. Perhaps even more than you do about yourself!" He continues, ignoring my dubious expression. "Small talk makes you crazy, so I'm going to get right to it. As shocking as my proposal is, I'm going to lay it out on the table and then give you the day to absorb it. I'm hoping you'll meet me for dinner tonight. You pick the restaurant."

"I can't meet you tonight." I start fidgeting. "I'm going to San Francisco for the weekend to celebrate my birthday. The second half of my life starts this year, so I'm tying up the loose ends and dusting out all the cobwebs from the first half. I'm moving into part two with a clean slate, as empty as possible." I tap my fingers.

"Keep me updated on your progress." Chip's blue eyes twinkle. "It might take longer than you think."

I let out a deep sigh of frustration. "Can you just get to it, please? In the words of Ambrose Bierce, 'Patience is a minor form of despair, disguised as a virtue.'"[24]

"Okay. Here goes." Chip rhythmically bangs a spoon on the side of his coffee cup saucer. I look at him. I look at the

---

[24] Ambrose Bierce, *The Devil's Dictionary*, originally printed in 1911, Cornell University Library, 2009.

spoon. He stops. "I've been sent to you as a messenger from my father, Lord of G.O.D., to hire you to do publicity and stuff for him... Well, for us."

"Us? I don't recall a Chip ever being mentioned in any Holy Scriptures."

"Well, G.O.D. isn't what you think it is either, but that's a story for another time."

"Publicity *and stuff*? Haha. Who put you up to this? So that's how you knew my name... Who's in on this with you? Great joke, but the jig's up!"

"Well, Lord did. We'll talk more about it later," Chip assures me, relishing a sip of coffee as he watches his words sink in.

"GOD WANTS ME TO WHAT?" I gasp. "What does he need a publicist for? He's GOD, for Christ's sake. I mean... YOU KNOW WHAT I MEAN! Couldn't he just toss an article or story anywhere he wants without much ado?"

"Not God, Lord. There's a difference," Chip states.

"Funny," I say, not laughing. "God wants a publicist? That's a good one."

"Lord." Chip corrects me again. "All your questions are reasonable." He calmly sips his other beverage. "Mmm. This fresh-squeezed grapefruit juice really hits the spot."

My eyes peruse the room. "Okay, I get it. Where are the TV cameras? Which reality show is this?"

"Funny you should ask." Chip chuckles. "It's REAL reality—the one and only reality. You know it's real because it doesn't go away once you stop believing in it."[25]

---

[25] Paraphrasing author Philip K. Dick in *I Hope I Arrive Soon*, 1985.

If there's an expression that displays disbelief mixed with Oh-my-God-if-this-is-really-true-it-would-be-so-incredible elation, I have it on my face.

Opening my mouth in an attempt to say something only produces a jumble of noises—all nice sounds, but nothing really amounting to coherence. Questions are racing toward my lips, each one trying to get out first, and yet, I don't know what to say.

Just then, my close friend Larry appears and I breathe a sigh of relief. We met years ago when we were both studying conspiracy theories and how to claim our rights as sovereign citizens.[26] Like clockwork, we each decided it was all too much hassle at the same time and moved on, but we've remained dear friends. We still like to discuss the workings of this place called Earth, though.

"Larry! What are you doing here? You're in on this, right?"

"Picking up lunch for the office. In on what?" Larry notices Chip. "Introduce me." Turning his attention back to me, he says, "I'm glad I ran into you. Big news to tell."

"Don't pretend you two don't know each other." I punch Larry in the arm. "You really had me going. God, am I a sucker. And what office? You have a new job?"

"What are you talking about?" Larry's doing a good job of acting confused, but I'm not buying it. "Hi, I'm Larry." He offers Chip his hand. "And you are?" He now seems to be completely oblivious to my presence.

---

[26] The sovereign citizen movement is a loose grouping of American and Canadian residents who feel they are answerable only to their particular interpretation of the common law, and believe the United States government is illegitimate. Wikipedia.

They haven't met. This isn't a setup. I'm not on a reality show. I get lost in my thoughts until Larry's voice pulls me out…

"Gotta run."

"Wait a minute! What job? What news?" I splutter as Larry leaves, gesturing for me to call him.

Chip gets back to business. "So, any more thoughts on what I said?"

"I thought for sure that when Larry walked up, the joke was about to be revealed." I gaze into Chip's eyes, looking for any sign of anything. "This isn't a joke, is it?"

"No, Sunshine. 'Fraid not."

Not quite believing what I'm hearing, I feel like someone who just scratched a winning lottery ticket but isn't sure if it's real. *Publicist for God?*

Still, I have a trip to San Francisco planned. And to show you how stubborn I am, and how easily and readily I can avoid absorbing what's happening, I insist on going. *The Lord's son can descend from heaven, invite me to breakfast, and ask me to work with him to change the world—but I have my plans, goddammit.*

"I'll call you," I say as I get up from the table. "This has been fascinating. Thanks for breakfast. Oh, and the name is Nanette, not Sunshine."

"Before you go…" Chip hands me a cell phone. "Here's the best way to reach me, Sunshine. Number's programmed in." He winks. I playfully stick out my tongue. "Call me any time, for any reason. We'll have that dinner when you get home." He brings his palms together on his chest and bows his head.

***

Meanwhile, plans for the upcoming weekend at The Bohemian Grove[27] start rolling out. "Larry get the list of invitees from Gil, forward the invitation, and plan for a trip to The Grove early next week," Cretin orders. "I need your help setting up a few things. You'll only be gone for one night. Here's the invitation."

Bohemian **B**rothers—**B**oard **M**embers
The Sun is once again swimming in the fishes
and the foreboding season of endings and
beginnings bids us to the forest—for two nights
only—to meet with the Night Eagle.

Be there Friday.

Gate opens at 1 a.m.
Arrive no later than 4 a.m.
Ceremony begins at 6 a.m. sharp.

---

[27] A 2,700-acre campground located in Monte Rio, California, belonging to a private San Francisco-based men's art club known as the Bohemian Club.

"I'd like to stay for the ceremony." Larry feels a little wobbly—this is one of the moments he has been waiting for. He heard rumblings of what happens at The Grove long before he started working for Cretin. He desperately wants to be privy to the occurrences at what they affectionately call "the encampment."

"Not a chance. But I take note of your enthusiasm."

"Thank you, sir."

Larry forwards the invite to the list as instructed. Surreptitiously, he sends Nanette a copy, too, the subject line reading: SURPRISE—URGENT!!!

We're going on a trip—short, sweet, and informative. Meet our private jet this coming Wed morning at 5 a.m. at the Van Nuys airport. I know it's early, but don't worry…BMOB!!![28]

Covering his tracks, he erases the email from the sent file. Inviting her to The Grove is a pretty big violation of trust for someone in his position. But they've been talking about getting in there for years. In Larry's mind, the accomplishment outweighs the risk.

---

[28] Bloody Marys on board.

nine

On the drive to the Bay Area to celebrate my forty-fifth birthday, I can't get Chip or the events of the previous day out of my mind. One minute I'm giddy, the next indignant. *How could anyone believe I'd fall for such a prank?* Not ready to talk about what's happening, I fantasize about the potential reality. At the same time, the thought makes me shudder.

I spend the weekend in San Francisco in a martial arts workshop, visiting friends, and seeing a nutritional scientist—an eccentric, ninety-year-old lady. She provides the results from her 100 hours of analysis of my urine to determine how to help with my chronic health issues: hepatitis C, diverticulitis, and asthma. A trifecta!

As planned, I spend the last night in the Bay Area at my friend Emily's house. She lives in Pacifica among the redwoods, surrounded by clean air, beautiful scenery, and no smog.

When I arrive at her house, all I want to do is go on a nice long walk with her, catch up, and chat about recent occurrences. I want to talk about all the shifts in my life since setting my new intention. Some pretty out-of-the-ordinary things have been happening and I'm interested in hearing her take on things. Forty-five starts part two, with a whole new playing field. Of course, I want to hear about her life, too.

Well, as often happens, things don't go quite as planned. Emily has two rambunctious children and they each have a friend over. There's no space for us to do anything alone. We all go for a walk...Emily, me, and four children between the ages of three and six. Intimate, deep conversation cannot happen under these conditions and I observe myself getting extremely frustrated. *Having a hissy fit just because I cannot blah, blah, blah.*

Then it hits me: I'm walking among exquisite redwood trees with some of my favorite people on the planet, and instead of enjoying the life-giving scenery and playing with the beautiful children, I'm upset because I'm not getting my way!

I wake up; I get it—on a deep level. I set a new reference point for acceptance, for allowing what's actually happening to happen and begin enjoying the moment. Instead of pouting, I throw down my ugly cloak of indignation and start chasing the kids. I consciously decide to have fun instead of being a shithead, and everyone is better off for it.

Presence. I'm grateful for the shift on many levels. I flash back fondly to Bella's insights on the beach.

We go back to the house and order Chinese food for dinner. My fortune cookie is prophetic: YOU WILL SOON WITNESS A MIRACLE.

We head to bed early, but once again, sleep doesn't bless me easily with so many thoughts and feelings rolling around my mind. The visit to the scientist, some things I learned in the workshop…including playing with peripheral vision instead of focused vision and a connecting concept called "allowing people to fall into my eyes." Everything—the past, the future. Life. Chip.

Time passes. Unable to sleep, but knowing I have a long ride and much work to do the next day, I find myself praying. "Please bring on slumber," I say audibly, not knowing who or what's listening. Almost instantly, something happens, as palpable as the sun's heat or its light reflected from the moon. I'm entranced. A voice booms in my head.

"Relax, Nanette. You are in the hand of God."

I drift off into sleep—deep, peaceful, and all-encompassing. I wake up the next morning in the same space...with an awareness of something bigger than myself and an experience of another dimension of reality.

I sigh. While other dimensions are beautiful spaces, I still have to pay rent and feed and clothe myself in this one, so I get into my car and head home. Refusing to spend the first day of the second half of my life on the boring, cow-dung-smelling Interstate 5, I take Highway 1, the Pacific Coast Highway. The drive's three hours longer, but a thousand times more beautiful.

The day is a stunning display of perfection: 78 degrees, azure sky, calm ocean. Driving along the coast, I spy the empty seat next to me, silhouetted by the shimmering sea. Who would I want with me on this day? Who do I know that could make this amazing time even better?

I ponder it deeply and come up with a profound answer: No one. Being extremely comfortable alone, I realize there's not one person I can think of on the planet who could make this day any better.

As good? Yes. Better? Nah.

This understanding blows me away. As I marvel in the truth of how much I enjoy being alone, here comes the voice.

"That's because you're not alone... You're with God."

"Great. I'm game," I say out loud to no one. "I'll spend my birthday with God." Perhaps I am talking to someone or something that I simply can't see. Either way, I find myself beginning to feel soothed by this newfound companion.

I continue down the road, stopping at Nepenthe for breakfast. One of the gems on Highway 1, Nepenthe is Big Sur's answer to Kauai's Napali coast. I order Eggs Benedict with real bacon—not that Canadian ham stuff they call bacon. I marvel at the incredibleness of this fine, fine day.

God doesn't order anything. Well…in truth, perhaps he orders everything.

After breakfast, walking down the stairs to my car, again I hear the quite persistent voice.

"God has a gift for you."

Obediently, I head to the gift shop, but it doesn't open for ten minutes. I check in with the voice and get the nod to leave Nepenthe, continue down the road, and wait for further instruction.

Before I know it, I find myself pulling off into a sweet little place called Harmony, California—a small artisan town that boasts a population of a whopping eighteen.

I receive the voice.

"See the glass blower in the back left corner of town? Go there."

By now a faithful servant, I head over to the shop. As I approach, I notice a man who could be Paul Newman's younger brother sitting next to a table with a well-worn red leather–covered Bible lying on it. I can tell this book has been read again and again and again.

I enter the store and wander around, enjoying all the beautifully hand-blown glass pieces. All the while, the man and I engage in small talk: The glass blower has been there for twenty years; he still comes in almost every day; and am I interested in anything in particular?

"Just looking," I tell him, abruptly blown away. A laminated sign stuck to the shelf in front of me quotes a Bible passage: YOU ARE NEVER ALONE.

The voice—and Chip—are gaining credibility by the minute.

"Turn around!"

I obey. My eyes are dazzled by a hand-blown glass ball, the likes of which I have never seen before. It's clearly a special piece kept in a separate case, the cosmos captured in 2 inches of roundness. The voice starts singing "Happy Birthday." It sounds like angels.

"I'll take it." I point to the orb. The man gets up slowly from his chair and ambles over. While removing it, he says, "This piece is special. I'm going to miss it."

"I know it is." I tell him bits and pieces of the story and how I was guided to the town, the store, and the orb.

When I finish, he points up and says tenderly and thoughtfully, "When you look up into the heavens, you know there has to be a Creator."

I stand there waiting for the voice to pick up the tab while the clerk waits for me to pull out my credit card. Since God apparently forgot his checkbook, I pay the $130 for my birthday present and head on down the road.

The voice whispers, "We'll get you later."

As it turns out, God is a great traveling companion. He never has to go to the bathroom, and is quite understanding when I do.

ten

Wandering around downtown Los Angeles, Chip is astonished. Earth's crowded. He doesn't remember so many structures, the place smelling so bad, or the air being so thick. Everyone's staring down into little rectangular boxes in their hands, not even acknowledging the others around them.

"What's happening on Earth?" He addresses a random person, who hands him a *Los Angeles Times*. The headline reads GLOBAL WARMING: TRUTH OR FICTION?

Chip looks up through the skyscrapers and all around, taking in the city from every possible angle. The air's clear from all the rain and the sun hot. *Global warming*? He ponders. *What would they have thought of the burning bush?*

Curious, dismayed, and amused all at once, Chip jumps on a bus heading toward Venice Beach. The ocean will be a perfect spot to figure out his game plan for bringing Nanette up to speed, reviewing the Law Book, and getting on with SpirIT's campaign to wake up souls.

"We need a catchy slogan…" He indranets Gabe as he gets lost in the scenery.

"Working on it," is sent back.

A disheveled man gets on the bus and sits down next to him, talking to himself.

Unflinchingly honest, Chip waves his hand in front of his nose. "Sir, you're quite odiferous. Do you need a few coins for a bathhouse visit?"

"Jesus is coming," says the man, battling imaginary insects with his arm.

"He is?" Chip decides to have some fun with the guy. "What's he gonna do when he gets here?"

"He died for your sins, you know. Jesus loves you." And in a moment of lucidity, he says, "Bathhouse? What century are you from? At least I know God. Jesus wouldn't care how I smell." The man brushes away one more unseen thing with his filth-streaked hand.

"Trust me, he does," Chip says under his breath as those nearby cover their noses and move as far away from him as possible, which isn't far.

The man gives Chip a Bible and gets off the bus. Chip opens the book to a random page and starts reading quietly to himself.

Isaiah 61:1–3: The Year of the Lord's Favor
The Spirit of the Sovereign Lord is on me,
because the Lord has anointed me
to proclaim good news to the poor.

"Quite the lofty language," Chip declares aloud. His outburst garners curious glances from the other passengers.

He has sent me to bind up the brokenhearted,
to proclaim freedom for the captives
and release from darkness for the prisoners,

That sounds like what I'm doing here! Chip laughs to himself. Freeing the prisoners of E.G.O. from this very book.

…to proclaim the year of the Lord's favor
and the day of vengeance of our God,
to comfort all who mourn,

"See? G.O.D. is being presented as an entity, rather than a Field," Chip remarks aloud. Someone sitting behind Chip moves to another seat while other passengers look at him out of the corner of their eyes. Chip looks around, flashes a beatific smile, and continues reading.

> ...and provide for those who grieve in Zion—
>   to bestow on them a crown of beauty
>   instead of ashes,
>   the oil of joy
>   instead of mourning,
>   and a garment of praise
>   instead of a spirit of despair.
> They will be called oaks of righteousness,
>   a planting of the Lord
>   for the display of his splendor.

"Wow," he says to no one in particular. "Wait until Lord hears of his desire to 'display of his splendor.' Talk about a self-centered divinity." Chip's awestruck by the masterful intertwining of the truth within the lie.

The synchrony of specific verses in relation to his personal mission on Earth causes him to wonder if Lord had a hand in choosing this passage—releasing the prisoners from darkness, bestowing oil of joy to the oaks of righteousness...

It's all about nature, he thinks. Everything is there.

Just then, he notices a tree with purple flowers on it and stands up to get off the bus to visit with it.

"Washington Street Pier!" the bus driver calls out.

Chip notices the synchronicity: his thought of nature, the lure of the tree, and being in the right place to get off the bus. He nods to The Field.

***

Lord feels Chip and *kvells*, happy the boy remembered and is activating "acknowledgement…only takes a wink or a nod to signal you've received IT's[29] offering."

***

Chip's eyes dart around in wonderment as he saunters toward the tree, all the while beaming love and admiration for its beauty and service. He picks a small branch with several flowers on it, then bends down and places his dolomite ring at the roots. "Thank you, sister," he says to the tree as he leaves.

"Excuse me, sir!" A woman catches his attention. "You left your ring there. I'd hate for you to lose it."

"Thank you, madam. It's an offering to the tree for this lovely twig." He holds up the branch adorned with an exquisite amethyst-colored flower. "Am I to expect to receive such beauty and pay no price?"

"Whatevs," she says and continues on her way, looking at him as if he's missing a few synapses.

Chip marvels at the large rear end of a cow protruding from the marquee of the Cow's End Coffeehouse. He pulls off his watch, snaps a photo, and sends it to Lord with a note: THIS PLACE IS UDDERLY DIVINE! I'M SO MOOOOOVED TO BE HERE.

Chip's not short on humor, either. He gets himself a coffee. So far he's found each cup is everything it's cracked up to be.

Venice Beach is electric. The place is hopping—people in every state of array and disarray, dancing, running, singing, begging, drumming, and roller-skating. *So much life!*

---

[29] SpirIT's nickname.

Chip's reminded once again of his life as Jesus as he examines the people lining the boardwalk, hawking all kinds of wares, tossing runes, and reading cards.

"Just like the temple… Some things never change," he says out loud, taking it all in.

A man, clearly overdressed for the weather in a green suit with large lapels, approaches. He smells of alcohol and body odor, the scent reeling Chip around just as the man taps him on his shoulder. "Hey, man, got any spare change? My car died and I need bus fare…"

"Is bathing verboten these days?"

"Funny, dude. Got any spare change?"

"How much is bus fare?" Chip pulls a handful of coins out of his pocket.

The guy sticks out his hand. "Hi, brother. I'm George Washington. Good to meet you. Bus fare to San Diego's forty bucks."

"Well, George, here's a little something to get you started on your journey home." The man spits on the ground while shaking the two dollars and change in his hand.

"You should be grateful, not indignant," Chip says. "Every journey begins with a small step."

Suddenly, a beautiful woman appears out of nowhere. "Scat," she says, giving the beggar a sour look. He wanders off.

"Was that really necessary? Telling someone to scat?" Chip is a bit mystified. "I appreciate your wanting to help me, but I'm quite sure I don't need it."

"I know that guy," the woman says, steamrolling her way into a conversation. "He doesn't have a car. He doesn't ride the bus. He bums money from people for drinks. Glad I could help." She sticks out her hand. "Hello, I'm Angel. Pleased to meet you. You're not from around here, are you?"

"I'm Chip, and I'm not."

"You're not pleased to meet me?"

"No, I'm not from around here. I don't know if I'm pleased to meet to you yet or not."

"Funny."

"You're mighty brazen. Is it your habit to get involved in matters of which you have no business?"

"Oh, we have business," Angel says. "Let's talk about it over coffee. Paschar told me you'd be coming, and to keep an eye on you while you're here."

Chip notices an instant pang of disbelief in his gut. Following his intuition, he declines the suggestion. "No thank you, but what a lovely invitation." Chip starts backing away. "Perhaps another time. I'll give your regards to Paschar."

He turns and weaves his way toward the sea through the bicycles, people, dogs, and surfboards, leaving Angel standing on the boardwalk amid the Tarot readers, sunglass salesfolk, and street performers.

Chip finds a spot near the water's edge, removes his shirt, and takes a deep breath. His lungs fill with ocean-fresh air. He sits down, rests his eyes, and relaxes into the sand, a look of contentment on his face as if he were cupped by the large hand of a loving mother. He lets out a deep sigh of relief.

As he returns from his relaxed state, he notices an attractive, middle-aged woman watching him. She's clearly mesmerized by his presence, which is not an uncommon reaction among earthlings. With his olive skin, dark hair, and blue eyes, Chip's truly a sight to behold.

"How are you?" he inquires.

"Enjoying this beautiful day!" she says, pausing. "There's something about you." She blushes. "You just look so content. And not bad on the eyes, either."

Chip looks down. "Women certainly have gotten brazen over the centuries," he remarks.

"I was just wondering if you're married."

"Well, no. But I am on a mission."

"Do tell."

"You're welcome to have a seat." Chip pulls a folded cloth from his bag and places it on the sand. He turns his hand over toward it, indicating it's for her. "I was just about to review some material. You may find it captivating, and I could use an audience."

"Yeah?"

"It'd be a big help if you ask me any questions that come up as I read. You game?"

"I've got a bit of time." She takes a seat on the colorful, hand-embroidered ground covering.

"Are you from here?"

"No, Colorado originally." She laughs. "But most people in Los Angeles are from somewhere else. I've lived here a long time, though."

"Well, I'm not from here either. I'm from a place called…" Chip tunes into Gabe for an answer and immediately receives: "…Canada. I'm from Vancouver, Canada."

"Nice. It's beautiful up there."

"What do you do here on Earth?"

"Here on Earth, I'm a life coach. On Venus, I'm a LOVE expert. On Mercury, I'm a messenger, and on—"

"Okay, okay!" Chip places his hand on her shoulder. "Point taken. What exactly is a life coach? Do people in this day and age need help living?"

"Well... I help people navigate life!"

"Good gig. So you've got this place all figured out, have you?"

"And you? What is it you do here on Earth?" she retorts, picking up some sand and letting it run through her fingers. "Or better yet, what planet are you from?"

"I'm from Canada..."

"Last time I checked, Canada's on Earth."

"Let's get to the material I mentioned, okay? Ready to listen?"

"I'm willing to listen, Mr. Here-on-Earth, but I already have questions."

"All will be revealed," Chip replies, "in good time."

He takes out the HOME Law Book, opens it to the first page, and begins reading.

"Welcome to the Galactic Order of Demonstration..."

eleven

The moment I get home, I want to contact Chip and tell him about my trip, but first I have work to do. I haul in my things, sit down at the computer, and immediately create a three-day menu for a client who's hired me as her personal chef. An email from Larry pops up with SURPRISE—URGENT!!! in the subject line. I call him.

"Happy Birthday, Nanette! Russian River! Cremation of Care!"

Larry's more excited than when we found out we got eighth-row-center seats to see Barbra.

"What? Are you kidding me? Shit! I can't go to Russian River—I just got back from the Bay Area! It's such short notice... There's so much to tell you."

"Nanette," Larry's voice stiffens, "this is what we've been waiting for! It's The Grove. This is our chance to explore... And I have a lot to tell you, too."

"Are we invited?"

"Well, not really. But my boss Cretin is sending me up there to do some setup. I'll book the hotel for an extra night and check out the lay of the land. We can sneak in the back and witness the ceremony for ourselves... How long have we wanted this?!"

"*Cretin* Cretin?"

"I told you I have a lot to tell you, too!"

"Risky. Real risky." Distracted, I look through notes, type a menu, and fully arrive back home during the conversation. "Scary, exciting, but risky... Wow, witnessing Cremation of Care. I can't believe I'm saying this, but I simply cannot go, even for a short trip. I have too much to do and have to follow my instincts on this one. My whole body is telling me no."

"Nanette, you *have* to come." His volume drops. He's clearly deflated.

"I'm so sorry, sweetheart, but you're on your own. I can't wait to hear about it. Ugh. The timing's just off and I must pay attention to that. I gotta run. I can't wait to hear about your job, too."

"Before you go, who was that guy you were with the other day?" Larry implores.

"Lots to tell," I say. "You'll never believe it."

"Okay, love. I'll miss you."

"Talk when you get back... STAY SAFE!"

twelve

Outside of the annual two-week gathering—where the future of the world is decided in clandestine meetings, effigies are burned, and more wine, women, and song flow than one could consume in a lifetime—it isn't often that a meeting is called at The Grove. The rarity highlights the importance of this event. Only the most elite of E.G.O. are invited, and The Grove's most famous rule, "Weaving Spiders Come Not Here,"[30] will be suspended; they are here to do the very thing the rule was created to curb, talk about business and plan the future.

Akin to a college fraternity, the one rule always strictly adhered to at The Grove is *everyone drinks*, so gin fizzes are traditionally served in bed at seven a.m. by camp valets. They'll also be handed to participants immediately upon arrival.

Bohemian Grove, known as The Grove for short, boasts the largest grove of old-growth redwoods in Sonoma County, some over 1,000 years old. The most powerful of powerful men—who, in actuality, run the world—meet there to celebrate art, music, nature, and each other... Oh, and to align their vision.

Larry arrives early. He's in awe of the grandeur of the grounds—prime real estate in the heart of lush Russian River Valley. Within seconds of pulling into the

---

[30] A phrase meaning, "No business is to be transacted." Business-Managed Democracy.

driveway, he's met by the head of security, the same as anyone who arrives.

"Good afternoon, Bricker." He sticks out his hand. "I'm Larry from the office. You're expecting me."

Bricker's a man of few words and big muscles. "Follow me."

The behemoth of a man escorts Larry to a small office carved into the trunk of an ancient redwood tree. "No walking around on the grounds unescorted," Bricker says. "Buzz me if you need anything."

"I can't do my work without access. Cretin wants me to set up hospitality, check on the theater, replenish the arts and crafts area, get the piano tuned... There's a lot to do."

Secretly, Larry hopes he'll have full run of the place. After all, he's Cretin's number one man. No such luck.

"I have a team of security personnel assigned to assist you with all your needs," the emotionless hulk replies. "Whenever you're ready, they will escort and assist you. I leave you to your work."

Disappointed the day isn't going to go as planned but excited to be there at all, Larry shrugs as he sets up his laptop, reviews his RSVPs, and prints out a guest list for the front gate security that reads like a Who's Who in world domination political theater.

MINISTER	INDUSTRY	INTERNAL DEPT.	PUBLIC NAME
Simeon Eadwig	Banking/Economics/ Insurance	Finance Control	World Banking Commission
George Giles	Taxation	Endless Paperwork	Internal Revenue Service
Elmo Hammond	Law/Military/ Prison/Firearms	Elite Order Protection	Public Safety
Janus Kiro	Media	Misdirection & Spin	Public Affairs & News
SakuDoka	Media	Misdirection & Spin	Entertainment
Gene Edicts	Science	Life Form Advancement	Scientific Advisory Committee
Monty Santo	Agribusiness	Earth Alteration	Environmental Protection Agency
Robert Slick	Petroleum	Elite Resources	Renewable Energy Resource Group
Will Gateways	Technology	Surveillance	Internet Oversight Committee
Leon Pius	Pharmaceutical and Street Drugs Tobacco/Gambling/ Alcohol	Addiction & Disease	Elite Health Administration
Hera Fortuna	Sex/Pornography	Immorality	Sex Education
Amos Duff	Religion	Mind Control	(Too many to list)
Sybil Veda	Academia	Misinformation	Education, Formation & Compliance

Larry walks outside the office and is immediately greeted by a guard. "Shall I call someone?" he asks with a touch of you-know-better-than-this in his voice.

"Yes. I'm ready. Thank you." Larry realizes that the head of security wasn't joking about attempting any walkabouts. "Please tell Bricker there's a piano tuner arriving in fifteen minutes."

"Done. What else can I help you with?"

"And give him this." He holds out the guest list.

"Done. Anything else?"

"I need to check the ceremony space, arts and crafts area, and the stage...as well as the kitchen."

The security guard radios Bricker. "Wait here. Your guide's on his way," he says to Larry, leaving him standing outside the redwood tree office.

Having noticed an intricate system of cameras throughout the property, Larry doesn't dare make a move. He simply takes in the beauty and sounds of the forest around him. Within moments, a young man rides up on a horse with another saddled horse in tow.

"I assume you ride. Cretin doesn't hire anyone who doesn't."

Larry jumps on the horse with a self-confidence seen only in a master. The horse immediately responds to his commands and they move as one.

"Yes, I do." Larry's intentionally smug. "I need to go to the kitchen first, please."

"Follow me," says the young man. "By the way, my name's Arame, and I'm assigned to you all day," he calls back over his shoulder.

Larry nods, his eyes darting around the grounds trying to catch a glimpse of anything mysterious. He particularly wants to see the Owl of Bohemia, the 40-foot concrete and wire statue he's heard so much about. He spots it out of the corner of his eye. It's as creepy and grand as he imagined. The Owl stands next to the famous lake, where the idea of Care is poled to its death and Lakeside Chats[31] determine the future of the world.

---

[31] "Lakeside Chats stimulate political and policy discussions among the men at The Grove, and serve the purpose of allowing consensual understandings to take shape," Peter Martin Phillips, "A Relative Advantage: Sociology of the San Francisco Bohemian Club," PhD thesis, Sociology, University of California, Davis, 1994, pp. 106, 111. Business-Managed Democracy. Herinst.org.

Arame clears his throat and rides his horse in a circle, strongly hinting that Larry get a little skip in his step. Larry returns his focus to his guide and together they ride down the flora-lined road and arrive at their destination.

"Call me if you have any needs or questions. Otherwise, I'll wait for you out here," Arame says. Larry climbs off his horse and heads inside.

Even for someone with his wealthy upbringing, the place is impressive. The kitchen is filled with an array of the finest equipment available. It's open and beautifully constructed for ease when working.

He's surprised to see Chef Ernie Imgassy, even though he knew the man would be preparing the weekend's meals.

"Wow, Chef Ernie!" Larry says before he can stop himself and greet the man appropriately. "Sorry, but you surprised me." He sticks out his hand. "Pleased to meet you. I'm Larry, Cretin's assistant."

"Yes, hello." Ernie's a well-known television chef, but Larry's never found him to be that impressive. In fact, Larry and Nanette dined in his restaurant one night. They didn't know the chef himself had cooked and sent the food back. It was flavorless.

"I have a few things I need to check, and then I'll be out of your way," Larry says.

Ernie ignores him while racing back and forth from the counter to a large steaming pot on the stove. "Parsley!" he reminds himself as he grabs a bunch and throws it in.

Larry opens the refrigerator. The shelves are lined with rare items, including the last remaining bottles of

French Heidsieck Monopole 1907.[32] There is caviar, the finest cheeses and fruits…and the liquor cabinet is no different. Rum created to mark the fiftieth anniversary of the founding of Tobago and Trinidad produced entirely by hand over a period of six years… The list of extra-ordinary options goes on and on. Whatever Bohemians desire will be their reality. After all, they decide reality.

Chef Ernie swoops by, reaches around Larry, and grabs a large bottle of fresh-squeezed lemon juice.

"Let me know if you need anything, Chef. I'm putting together a list of final needs for Bricker."

"Thanks, Barry," Chef says, pouring the lemon juice into a blender. "I take care of myself."

"Ahh, it's Larry."

Ernie nods as if he cares, which he doesn't. Larry instantaneously decides not to let the glorified cook ruin his day as he heads from the open kitchen into the great room.

Beautiful light streams in through a mosaic-like wall created out of window sashes. They're made of all shapes and sizes that are artfully interspersed with stained-glass windowpanes that cast different hues on the room depending on the time of day. Turkish carpets made of the finest silk pile cover the floors. The feeling is of art and elegance combined. The room could not be more exotic, inviting, or comfortable.

Larry plops himself down in a wingback chair made of pure aniline leather. He takes inventory, making sure everything's in perfect order for the weekend's events:

---

[32] Champagne that was found in a century-old shipwreck in the late 1990s, valued at $25,000 a bottle.

"Firewood stocked—check. Delicacies—check. Vases filled with white lilies, roses, and lilacs—check."

Scanning the exquisite room, his eyes dart from one rare antiquity to another. The only five Gurkha Black Dragon Tubo cigar boxes still in existence, made out of camel bone and brass, are strategically placed around the room. They're to be filled with a combination of the toughest-to-find cigars in the world, including the last 900-year-old Mayan *sikars* on Earth. They run around $200,000 apiece.

And if the Bohemians want a group smoking experience, off to the right of the great room is a private space dedicated to one item: a 1,600-pound cigar called the Gran Habano. Forty people can smoke it simultaneously through a tubing system. Talk about male bonding!

Larry checks his list; everything here is finished. Just before leaving, he calls Arame to turn on the sound system for a check. Suddenly, the room's filled with magic. His body feels as if it's being carried away on a carpet of ultimate resonance.

"What is it about the sound in here?" he asks Arame.

"The room's a perfect acoustical sound chamber."

The more time Larry spends at The Grove, the more he understands the lure of the ranks of E.G.O.'s hierarchy. With every need catered to, their loyalties grow toward E.G.O. and away from their own innate powers, as well as decency and compassion. Life in the Elite Global Order is seductive.

thirteen

Lord's multifocus is on Chip, Gabriel's exclusive Map class
for their team of angels, Nanette, and Cretin's movements on
Earth—among other things. Being Lord equips him with
peripheral vision beyond human comprehension.

Chip's on the beach, and by now he's accumulated quite
a crowd. Lord observes as he teaches.

***

"G.O.D. is what?" someone yells from the crowd.

"It's the Galactic Order of Demonstration, essentially an
interactive field," Chip answers.

A haze of disbelief mixed with wonderment fills the
space.

"The whole point of having your mind blown is to open
it." Chip bends over and picks up a sand dollar. "Don't try
too hard to make sense of what you're hearing. New material
doesn't fit into old thought forms."

He holds up the sand dollar and crumbles it. "Let the
new information plant itself like a seed in the soil of your
consciousness. Observe its growth. Allow yourself to simply
contemplate what you're hearing." Chip walks toward and
into the water. Well, it's difficult to tell if he walks in it or on
it, but as he exits the sea, his feet aren't wet.

"Don't believe anything I tell you. Live with it and
determine for yourself if it's correct through your own
experiences. That's the difference between blind faith and
faith."

"Where can I find you?" a man says as the crowd cheers.

"More will be revealed," Chip assures them. "This isn't
the last time you'll see or hear from me. I promise."

He hears murmurs as they waft up from the crowd.

"Don't I know him?"

"He reminds me of someone."

"All will become clear in time." Chip holds his arms up, Jesus style. "Do not try. Don't try to understand. Trying is a mind game." He brings his arms down slowly. "You're a field, and whatever you plant, grows. Remember, acceptance is a planted seed sprouting in The Field of Awareness and it is the first step on the path to deliberate demonstration. Remember, keep your minds open!"

Rishi listens, rapt with awe. "How do I get in touch with you? I have a friend I want you to meet. By the way, I'm Rishi." She sticks out her hand. Chip cups her hand in his and receives her.

"I'm in between places right now. Don't worry, my new friend Rishi. We'll meet again."

***

Lord, enjoying some alone time in his private control room, feels confident with Chip's management of earthly affairs, so he turns his attention to Gabe and the Map. Intrigued, he heads over to the classroom to join the team in all his Lordness.

The Map Gabe created is the most reliable method ever conceived for tracking Earth denizens.

Lord enters just as Gabe begins the section on uses for the Map.

"You can find out anything—from how many people ate peanut butter yesterday to how many souls are in which court." Gabe flashes through various screens, pointing out their features. "I'm working on the Team AWE Broadcasting system. It's just now ready for testing."

"Nice," says Paschar. "This will make our jobs so much easier."

"Not only will we be able to track souls—and their moods and tones…" Gabe taps some buttons and the screen turns to sultry colors. "…we'll also be able to dispatch messages to Team AWE at a moment's notice. It's going to revolutionize the Awakening."

"The what?" Lord asks.

"Well, I had to call it something."

"Let us call it AWE-wakening." Lord's eyes twinkle. "It sounds less like the second coming, and besides, it is what is actually happening: we are waking up AWE."

"AWE-wakening it is!" Gabe claps his hands together once. "I like it."

"And we can refer to the team as AWE-wakeners. Carry on, Gabe."

Lord claims an empty desk in the back of the classroom. His focus is now on Nanette. He carefully reviews the first law of demonstration, *acceptance*, considering the next overstanding she needs to have woven innately into her awareness in order to be "drawing from the divine pool of wisdom" with every word, thought, and deed. To become a walking demonstration of demonstration—a tall order for anyone, really.

"We have to run an ASK/GET!" Lord blurts out, interrupting Gabe. "Accepting and using the earthly workings of ASK/GET is a crucial tool for demonstrating. This is a fortunate event!"

Lord raises his index finger in the air. "An opportunity to show the angels how to use the Map *and* test Team AWE Broadcasting with an authentic programming. I will be back in a jiffy." Lord disappears in a puff of smoke.

"This is unprecedented," Gabe tells the angels. "You're the first beings outside of the inner circle to have a live demonstration of how the Map works, let alone observe a test run of a new advancement. Learning the Map is vital to our important mission."

Excited at the news, the angels' wings spontaneously expand and fill the space.

Lord sweeps into the room as a fireball. The angels pull their wings back in just in time to avoid catching fire. He lands in his seat and changes back into his previous form.

Needless to say, our overseer has dramatic flair.

"Okay, Gabe. Ready?"

Gabe nods.

"Here we go…GL74321–43, HC22572–71, DP94523–12…"

The numbers being read off are a list of coordinates. Various points on the Map illuminate in different color sequences until a final triple flash of the lights and a sound of heavenly trumpets blares through the room.

"Beautiful touch, but turn it down a bit." Lord lowers his own voice as he speaks. Gabriel beams as he adjusts the volume.

"What just happened?" Michael asks.

"The flash signals confirmation that these important directions have been received by those needing to receive them. The trumpets mean all systems go." Gabe blushes. "I LOVE heavenly trumpets."

"What did you put into place, Lord?" Colopatiron asks. "What has begun?"

"Right now I am in the process of Nanette's Consciousness Competency Testing. We need to know how much of her lifelong training has actually been absorbed." Lord raps his knuckles on his head. "Hopefully something has sunk in."

"What's she being tested for?" Nathaniel asks.

"The embodiment of ASK/GET. It requires an understanding of how Field Prompts operate. Watch, listen, and learn."

"Can you give us specifics?" Paschar asks.

"**A**lways **S**eek **K**nowing, **G**ain **E**ternal **T**ruths," Lord offers, winking at Gabe.

Feeling a bit proud that Lord has embraced the acronym he coined, he says, "And E.G.O. has twisted around the meaning of prayer... They've taught humans that the law of ASK/GET is a petitioning system to this rewarding/punishing entity they created called 'God.' It's no wonder earthlings are so out of sync with the natural laws."

"Well spoken. Now, angels, watch and determine if, when, and how Nanette demonstrates an understanding of ASK/GET."

Gabe tunes the Map to Nanette at her house. She's standing in her kitchen, frenetically mincing garlic and ginger.

"I will be back soon," Lord says. "Pay attention!"

With that, he heads out to the garden and peruses other information on his portable Sheet of the World.

fourteen

My head swirls as I prepare three days of food, nine different meals, to deliver to my client. As usual, I'm pondering life, especially since the latest developments in mine have given me a lot to contemplate. My life flashes before my eyes, all the mystical experiences, insights, disappointments, joys, difficulties—everything.

Has my whole life been a period of training for this moment? Do I have a willful imagination, or am I being courted by the most powerful of all powers? Is it time to get happy? And why is Larry getting into The Grove all of a sudden? I mean, why now?

Ginger root and garlic mince into tiny pieces beneath my blade as I contemplate the first day of the second half of my life. Truly cosmic—a day led by following! What's the deeper meaning of the message, "You are never alone; you're with God?" Not being a moron, I get it, but I don't get it at the same time.

Does it actually apply to my life? How does this message help me feel more comfortable being alive? What does this have to do with completing the unfinished business from the first half of my life? Or is this about how to proceed in the future? Who or what is this voice that speaks to me? And what does Chip have to do with all this?

Moving on to the carrots, I chop in wonderment of the future, the past, and the present. So many questions. So few answers. Perhaps one answer is in the way this precious day unfolded.

I allowed something else besides myself to guide me, I muse. I paid attention to an inner voice—one that's seemingly connected to a bigger picture. I surrendered to something, an inner authority. *Maybe I just need to get out of my own way.* Allow good to unfold as it appears to be…

As I weigh getting out of my way, I smell something burning.

Shit. I throw the pot of burned rice into the sink. Apparently, I can only get so far out of my own way without ruining a meal. Or maybe there's more for me understand. All I know is nobody wants to eat overcooked anything. *Maybe I'm overcooking myself.*

Flustered, I complain, "Does every single iota of an event have to have some deeper meaning? Is everything a fuckin' message? Can't something just burn?"

The expulsion of profanity offers me a sense of relief. I literally exhaust myself! *Can't I shut this mind off?!*

I continue talking. "'You're never alone' is a nice metaphor, Voice, but where's the help when I really need it? Like getting this food cooked and delivered. Real life, real help. Voice? God?! Answer me that. Put up or shut up!"

The phone rings.

My friend Rishi's voice spills into my ear. "Hey, honey. I'm in the neighborhood with some time to kill. I was just wondering if you need any help."

"YES! I do."

Ten minutes later, she appears at the door, her green eyes and auburn hair shining in the sunlight.

The moment has not been lost on me. "Rishi, thank God you called," I say with a bit of awe. "I need so much help right now, I don't know what I would do without you!"

"Did I hear you say, 'Thank God'?"

The voice in my head teases and I feel what I equate to the hand of God giving me an internal love tap (whack) upside the inside of my brain.

"Didn't you ask for help, Nanette?"

Who knew "I told you so" is also God's creation?

Rishi puts down her knapsack and a big box, and then takes off her shoes. She pets and says hello to my cat. "Map Meop," Olivia the feline answers, saying "hi" back. She shimmies her tail.

"You know, I was on my way home, but I got this strong urge to call you. It almost felt like a directive."

"Funny, I was just contemplating the implications of the lesson 'You are never alone,' and you show up. You haven't heard that story yet. Something's going on."

Rishi hands me the box. "Oh, by the way—Happy Birthday!"

I didn't see the red bow before. "Thanks, love. I'll open it later, okay? I've got to focus." I put the box down.

"What can I do to help?"

"Would you put on a pot of rice? I'll run downstairs to the garage and get some containers for packaging."

"You got it." I hear the water turn on. "Use a cup of chicken broth, top shelf—fridge," I holler.

"Got it! I can't wait to tell you about this guy I met at the beach," she yells over the sound of running water. "You'd love him... I love him!"

"Can't wait," I say. "I've met someone interesting, too. Actually, he's beyond interes—"

Paying more attention to the conversation than the steps, I slip down the last four, breaking the momentum of the fall with my right wrist—the hand I use for everything.

I can immediately feel it starting to swell.

"Shit," I scream. "SHIT!"

Rishi comes running downstairs. "What happened?"

"I fell."

Rishi holds me by the arm and help me upstairs. I'm a bit wobbly, nauseous, and disoriented, and my wrist is growing bigger by the minute. It's all I can do not to vomit and I feel as if I might pass out.

Concerned with my wrist's rapidly swelling appearance, my friend wants me to go the hospital. "You'd better get that checked." She's not kidding, and is trying to scare me into compliance with her concerned facial expressions and intentional tone.

"I don't have time for this!" I yell, strongly refusing. "The novices are just back after a three-week break. I can't take the day off. I don't want to take the day off! I need my wrist better by tomorrow."

"Hospital!" she insists.

"Nope, not going to the hospital," I say. "I'm going to follow my intuition on this one. I'm getting a message."

"I've got a message for you!" Rishi growls. "Your stubbornness is showing."

"I know what I've got to do. I've been following something lately... I'll tell you more about it later. I need a nap."

"Do whatever it is you need to do. I'm here to help, not to judge." She kisses me on the forehead. "I'll call your client, explain what happened, and let her know the food will be later than usual."

"Great." I kiss Rishi on both cheeks. "I'm so grateful. Thank you."

"Go take your nap. I'll take care of everything." Rishi pulls the rice off the stove and fluffs it with a fork. "You're so welcome, my friend."

I close my eyes, breathe a sigh of relief, and head to my bedroom. Rishi follows me, covers me with a blanket, and then leaves me to rest. I hear her finish packing the food and the door close.

I quiet myself, connect with the voice, and ask, "What's the fastest way to heal this wrist?" Within moments, I hear,

"Tape five pennies on the bottom of your wrist and two pennies on the top. Sleep with it that way and it will heal quickly."

After that, silence.

"What the hell," I mumble to myself. "It cain't hoit."

I get myself the prescribed number of pennies, some medical tape, and an ace bandage. I fix myself up and doze off into much-needed sleep.

***

I'm half-asleep with the television on when two news anchors talking about the upcoming TASTE Conference pulls me out of a dreamy state. Suddenly, I'm wide awake.

"News crews will not be allowed inside, but here's what we know so far..." Speculating about the event, broadcasting on and on.

"We have it from a good source that Angel, Cretin's wife, will be introducing some new programs."

Her photograph appears onscreen.

"I knew it. I KNEW it!" I scream. "I always said she was aligned with darkness."

I met Angel years ago, before she met Cretin. We were briefly friends. I should put the word friends in quotation marks because Angel isn't friends with anyone. Everyone's a means to an end.

When I let her know I didn't appreciate something she did that I felt was incredibly wrong, her response was, "God put me in your life to bring up your issues."

That's when I decided that if the devil were to incarnate on Earth, he would appear as a beautiful blonde called Angel who talks about God a lot, but alas, with an ugly agenda.

Time to get up. Life's calling me into action.

***

By the time Rishi returns from delivering the food, I'm
sitting in the kitchen savoring a cup of Kukicha[33] tea. I point
to the pot.

"How's your wrist?" She sits down and pours herself a
cup.

"Surprisingly much better!"

"Did you do anything besides wrap it?" she asks with an
eyebrow raised. Rishi has known me a long time and has
been through some humdingers with me. Once I attempted to
heal an ear infection by sticking a clove of raw garlic in my
ear, but then couldn't find it. I thought it got lost inside my
head. She went with me to the doctor, who said the garlic had
inflamed my inner ear and must have fallen out when I
wasn't looking.

Not one of my finest moments.

"Uh-huh. Taped pennies to it."

"Really." She rests her chin on her palms and her elbows
on the table.

"Yep. It'll be good as new by tomorrow."

Rishi shoots love at me from her eyes then reaches for
the box. "I can't wait for you to see your present!" She hands
it to me. "Open it!"

The box is big, but lighter than a feather. I can't imagine
what's inside. Humming to the tune of Jeopardy's final
question, I unwrap it with one hand.

"Twenty Spanish lessons!" I scream and her face lights
up. "Online with Tatiana! *Gracias!* I'm so excited. I can't
wait to get started. How'd you get in touch with her?"

---

[33] Kukicha, also known as twig tea, is a Japanese blend made of stems, stalks, and
twigs.

97

"From a group email you sent us. We met once on Skype during one of your famous ceviche pisco sour parties. By the way, not a bad way to say thanks for your help!" She winks. "That kick-ass kimchi you make wouldn't make me sad, either."

"Right. Right, you got it!" I say. "Boy, do I want to go back to Peru. And to be there and speak the language more fluently…" My mind wanders off to the Andes for a minute, then floats back at the sound of Rishi's voice.

"Anyway, let me tell you about this guy I met," she says. "It was like it was meant to be or something."

"Stories with the words 'it was meant to be' always sound so fated and romantic. Where'd you meet him? We'll have to invite him over for ceviche!"

"At the beach the other day… I don't think I've ever met anyone the likes of this man. I noticed him, he noticed me, we chatted for a minute, and then he asked for my ear and started reading to me from this beautiful book he was carry- ing. People gathered… As I listened, I kept getting flashes that you two should meet. I told him I had someone I wanted to introduce him to, and he said we'd meet again for certain. And then he left without exchanging any info! Odd."

"He was confident. And the book he read from…simple, yet so poignant."

"Really." I stare at her as a strange sensation tickles the insides of my gastrointestinal tract. "Interesting."

"Come on," Rishi says. "Your turn!"

"Okay. I can't believe we haven't spoken since court."

"Me either. What happened?"

"After winning my case?" I rock from side to side enthusiastically.

"Congratulations!" Rishi high-fives me. "You were so confident…that's a lesson in something."

"Beyond being a lesson, it's a new reference point." A calm stillness fills me.

"New reference point? Sounds good. What's that?" My friend loves new tools for the "life toolbox."

"In the past, I might have caved to everyone else's opinion, even though I had such a strong inner knowing that I should fight the ticket. I would've felt stupid for what I wanted to do and would've gone to traffic school. Instead, I followed my guidance, and it paid off. So I've got a new reference point for not disregarding myself. When similar situations come up, instead of snapping back or referring to childhood experiences, where I didn't trust myself or had to fight to be heard, I now have a new place to land—one where I listen to my own inner voice instead of everyone else's louder outside voices, and it works out."

"Ha! You go, girl! That's a beautiful teaching."

"Did I mention I won my case?"

She nods. "I believe you did."

"So, I walk out of the courthouse and meet this man who invites me to breakfast. I was up for an adventure, and since we were in a public place and I felt plenty safe, I accepted the offer. Crazy thing is, this guy knows my name, where to find me, and he tells me— Are you ready? No, really, are you ready? He says he's here to hire me to do publicity for God."

"Huh?"

"Why, that's exactly what I said!"

"Go on," she says. "I got goosebumps." She extends her mottled arm before me.

"He told me not to talk about it, but you're my best friend. And who knows if this is even real?" My eyes widen. "You have to meet him. I'm going to call him right now and tell him to come over."

***

"Jesus is Just Alright," Chip's favorite Doobie Brothers song and current ringtone, interrupts the laughter and screams as he runs around with a group of young children in a local park. He steps over to the side and answers it.

"Sunshine! Great hearing from you! Is this your call groveling for the job?" Chip teases. "You know, after all your divine encounters over the last few days?" He tosses a ball back toward a young girl and shares in her joy when she catches it.

"You've certainly caught my attention, Hey-sus. And remember, you came to me, not vice versa," Nanette says. "So you do the groveling. Anyway, come over right now! My best friend's here. I want you to meet her."

"My, aren't we assuming?" Chip chides.

"I mean, are you available to come over?"

"When I said you were assuming, I was talking about you inviting your friend into the mix without talking to me about it first, not about demanding me to come over *now*. I like your spunk *and* for the time being, let's keep this between the three of us, okay? See you in fifteen."

***

The door's wide open when Chip arrives, so I yell for him to come in without getting up. He walks in and throws a hardbound copy of the Bible at me. I instinctively catch it with my sprained right hand.

"What's this for? Never read it, never will." I put it down.

"You enjoy fiction, no?" he says. "How's the wrist?"

At his question, I realize I caught the book with the hurt arm. I look at my wrist, at the Bible, then at Chip.

"Seems pretty good, still hurts a little." I move my wrist around a little as I talk. "How'd you know about that?"

"How could your wrist possibly be so much better?" Rishi says, joining us from the bathroom.

"That's what happens when you ask and listen. You demonstrate healing."

"Chip! What are you doing here?"

"Hello, my sweet Rishi," he says. "Remember what I said? Alas, we meet again."

"I see you've already met Nanette."

"The friend you mentioned? It figures," he says with a twinkle.

"Why does it figure?"

"When one's InFlow, Earth experiences align with simple ease. When one isn't, ease doesn't exist in the area one is resisting. Meeting Nanette's best friend at the beach is what I would call being InFlow! After all, it's now clear you're also a vital part of this plan. More on that later."

"What plan?" Rishi asks. "And what's God like?"

"Well, that's the big question, isn't it? Actually, Lord is my father. He's head of G.O.D.—which isn't what you've been taught. I touched on it on the beach, remember?"

"You said a lot of things on the beach."

"Yes, I did. By the way, so good to be with you again."

Thus is how life on the planet Earth is designed to work.

fifteen

"Are you all watching Nanette?" Lord joins them again in the classroom. "What has she demonstrated so far?

"More than one ASK/GET in this scenario!" Colopatiron says. "Rishi showing up, the medical advice—"

"There is an important distinction here," Lord interrupts. "Rishi showing up was not the direct result of ASK/GET. Anyone know why?"

"It was a synchronistic event," Paschar jumps in. "Acknowledgement that Nanette followed earlier prompts." She stands up in her chair, pretending she's a preacher. "She was interacting with The Field regarding a previous lesson, assimilating 'You are never alone'—our girl was already in a demonstration cycle. Can I get an amen?"

"A-men" wafts through the halls of CPR.

"*Ding, ding, ding!*" Lord touches his nose. "Do say more…"

"Without having any clue, Nanette applied the Seven Attunements of Demonstration to the Field Prompts she received when she needed sleep. She *asked* for help, *accepted* direction, and paid *attention*."

Lord gives Paschar a thumbs-up and she continues. "She *acknowledged* The Field for its help, and her dedicated listening *allowed* her to be InFlow all day. She received synchronicity as acknowledgement of her committed participation, which is how human beings are rewarded for demonstrating…which is the only prayer, right? She allowed herself to be guided without resisting."

"A true feat for her, by the way," Lord says, boasting a bit about his fine work. He waves his arm and white doves and red-winged blackbirds fly out of nowhere, filling the space. They vanish, leaving an aviary-style untidiness.

Calissa, Lord's personal valet, shows up right on cue carrying a fairy-sized broom. She's wearing her favorite tiny majorette boots, complete with tassels, and has opalescent, dragonfly–like wings that glimmer in the light. She flips a switch and the room's built-in vacuum turns on, immediately pulling in some of the mess.

As she guides feathers toward the suction and flits here and there, Lord sneezes. Somewhere on Earth, a piece of toast dons a burn mark that looks like Jesus.

"She acknowledged the lesson 'You are never alone' and contemplated it," Paschar continues. "Nanette wanted to *assimilate* it—discover how literal or figurative 'the Voice' was regarding this particular message. She's working on the *appreciation* piece... However, she is in *awe* of her life right now."

"Shock is probably more the word," Lord poses. "She's receiving and transmitting with us at a whole new level, and still has no idea what is happening or what is in store for her. Ooooh! It is so exciting that it sends shivers of delight up and down my spine."

Everyone in Lord's presence swoons. And all creatures on Earth, no matter which side they're on, and if only for a moment, collectively feel it.

Gabriel's Sheet of the World glows with golden, opalescent hues. When earthlings attune, sounds that are too beautiful, too inspiring, and too revealing to reveal echo throughout the cosmos. SpirIT radiates sheer delight. As the tuning entity, IT loves good vibrations.

The room, now fully charged with energies of the finest quality, takes on a silky feel. Basking in total equilibrium is one of those moments that make being on Lord's intimate team particularly special.

Lord manipulates the vibrations into patterns of beautiful light dancing all around them. Barbra Streisand's voice floats in, singing "I'm in the Mood for Love." He loves Barbra.

"See the Map," Lord says. "It shows what is possible on Earth: complete attunement in LOVE. But it has to come from within each soul. When denizens of the planet reach a tipping point, LOVE will permeate their senses. It will be the lens through which they take action. The Golden Law will prevail. 'Do unto others…'"

Everyone pauses and appreciates the possibility of a planet where people live in LOVE.

An obvious chill shoots through Lord's body. "And LOVE never needs to be qualified with the word 'unconditional.'" He gets serious. "It is inherent. What earthlings are trying to do, when they qualify their love, is attempt to raise the vibration of their E.G.O.-fueled expression of acknowledgement for reciprocation or desire of mutual satisfaction to the level of the field of pure G.O.D.-LOVE. Even that, for most human beings, is an expansion of their usual state."

"Anything else, Paschar?"

"The medical advice…" Lord's Angel of Vision rolls into a somersault, landing with one knee up, one knee on the ground, and her arms open. "…was clearly ASK/GET. Nanette needed to know something, so she asked The Field and received an immediate answer. By asking and taking action on the answer she received, she demonstrated acceptance of The Field. Demonstration is always rewarded. And demonstration is the only prayer."

"You have been studying," Lord says. "Well done." A playful sort, he plucks a gold star out of midair and sticks it on Paschar's forehead. "You have demonstrated, and you are being rewarded."

"Oh, Lord," she blushes. A flash of electric blue light shoots from her psychic 'third eye.' "Earthlings so easily and often slough off the responses they are given to questions they ask because the answers are unexpectedly simple, or they expected them to arrive in a different package. Of course, whether or not the pennies will really work," Paschar says with a glint in her eye, "remains to be seen. I know she's shown some improvement but…she needs to be able lift heavy pans by tomorrow!"

"Are you doubting 'the Voice'?" Lord says. "There are penalties!"

Lord projects an image of the angels dressed in black and white stripes, wings intact, cleaning the Lord's silver—one of the most hated jobs. So tedious!

"Never!" the angels chime in.

"Well, by Earth standards, the cure is seemingly impossible," Michael comments. "How could taping pennies to it possibly do anything in terms of healing her wrist?"

"Exactly," says Nathaniel. "Which is why I find this so exciting." He claps his hands together.

"The fact is that this girl actually listens to the messages, and often demonstrates at lightning speed. You weren't kidding when you said you've been grooming her. She's perfect for the job." Gabe shoots a lightning bolt from his fingertip, illuminating his point.

He's CPR's resident "sky artisan." It's an exalted position. Designing sunrises, sunsets, and cloud formations is a post anyone would be excited to fill, and Gabe has always demonstrated excellence in The Field.

A smattering of applause emanates from the group.

"Well, she is a feisty one," Lord says. "For instance, sometimes she will resist things simply to resist them, not because she disagrees. It is a mechanism so engrained into her being that often, she does not even realize she is doing it. And irreverent? Whew!" He swipes the back of his hand across his forehead. "Finally—finally!—she has been moved by reverence. So now we are, at least, blessed with a range of disdain and awe…"

He reflects. "We should have made that teaching available sooner." He places his hands together in the prayer position and points them upward. "She's so much easier to be around." The angels put their hands together, too, and extend them toward Lord.

"So, she passed the initial listening tests, and even though she hasn't accepted the position, training mode has begun. Right?"

"Exactly, Gabriel," Lord replies. "Except, trust me, the position is hers. She just does not know it yet! It is all systems go."

"Anything else?" Gabe asks.

The flamboyant overseer nods and stands up. "Pay close attention to what I am about to tell you, because it is a vital overstanding for this mission," his eyes twinkle.

On the Map of the World, he shows a video presentation of the Palace of Knossos. Beautiful frescoes, ornate floors, and ancient olive oil jars offer scenes of life during the Minoan civilization. The last few scenes spotlight the still-solid foundation of the palace.

"Knossos on the Isle of Crete is considered the oldest city in Europe, and the foundation stands strong to this day. A solid foundation is the key to a lasting structure." He kicks the leg of the wooden table next to him. "Clearly built to last…"

He looks around to be sure he has everyone's full attention.

"Remember, team, once an incorrect or weak foundation is laid, all assumptions from that time forward are based on faulty premises. If the accepted belief about God is incorrect, then all systems springing from that belief are also incorrect. It is no mistake that the word 'lie' is embedded in the word 'belief.'

"Oh boy, we have work to do. First, we must alert earthlings to the misunderstandings they have accepted as truths. Reality will completely unravel their foundations, so re-pouring them is the heart of our work. We have to reframe the future, demonstrate truth... Construction metaphors just work so well when it comes to discussing our path."

"Daunting," Gabriel thinks aloud while Lord's projection on the wall shifts to a vision of a beautiful Eden-like garden and fills the room with the scent of freesias and hyacinths.

"This is not a linear process." Michael breathes in the fragrance. "A lot of change will happen at once."

Lord's map projection changes to smoke-bellowing factories, polluted rivers, and clear-cut forests. "E.G.O. promotes division, so instead of 'Playing The Field of Earth's Gifts,' earthlings drain her of her resources. People are driven to fight among themselves about who has the best god, the best politics, the most money... Gabe, take a note: 'Play The Field.' That is our slogan!"

"I LOVE it!" he agrees, shooting Chip a message. "Your son already asked about having one..."

"Instead of playing The Field and allowing themselves to be guided," Lord continues, "earthlings are driven to live in a static structure they call life! They move along on a nice little conveyor belt laid out for them. Along the way, their choices direct the conveyor belt, giving the appearance of freedom. I have been contemplating it since the download of information from the Akashic records. It is a rabbit hole."[34]

Everyone nods.

The picture on the wall changes to an empty, grass-filled field. Suddenly, a cartoon wabbit eating a carrot pokes his head out of an up-until-now-unseen opening and waves his paw.

"Once we deliver the laws, we will have to reiterate, again and again, that being awake is so much more desirable than being deceived. The more earthlings uncover and trust the authority within themselves to transmit with and receive from IT and The Field, the quicker Earth life will unfold as planned: A fun, challenging adventure filled with awe. But earthlings' beliefs are so deeply embedded. They will not change overnight." Lord shows the classic picture of apes evolving into man and takes an affectionate bow.

"Earth life is the best treasure hunt in all the multiverses combined…if one takes the time to embody, demonstrate, and acknowledge what they receive, no matter what is going on in EGOland. It is liftoff!"

Overjoyed with anticipation, the team joins hands and dances in a circle.

"It can be said," Lord offers, "that E.G.O. life is driven. G.O.D. life is guided."

---

[34] To go down a figurative never-ending tunnel with many twists and turns, never truly arriving at a final destination—just finding more tunnels.

sixteen

"Anyone want anything to drink?" Nanette yells from the kitchen.

"I'm good for now, thanks." Chip sits down.

"I'll have lemonade," Rishi shouts. "It's delicious," she adds to Chip. "I recommend it."

"Okay, make that two," he calls. "Then let's get to the reason we're all here, and what you're going to be doing for the next galactic week."

***

I bring the lemonade in and sit down. "Do Rishi and I have plans we don't know about?"

"Always," Chip says, grinning from cheek to cheek. "Always." He takes a sip and gets serious. "Uh, what makes this so good?"

"Not telling! I've got some secrets, too, ya know."

"Touché." Chip appreciates the humor. I shoulder-shimmy and sit up straighter.

"Okay, ready for a little learning?" He settles into his seat and pulls some papers out of his bag. "How about an introduction to the mystical field of demonstration?"

"Has anyone ever said no to that question?" Rishi asks.

I love her.

Our new friend looks my way with a quizzical expression...

"Of course I'm game." I walk over to the mantel, pick up the glass orb I got for my birthday, and then sit back down. "I have to admit that ever since I set the intention of completing the first half of my life, some all-knowing guide seems to have moved into my brain. When I listen to it and relax, everything works out with ease. When I try to figure things out, I get stuck. It's mind-blowing! Messages come to me from everywhere."

I hold up and move the light-refracting ball around, allowing the sunshine to strike it from all directions. Rainbows shoot around the room.

"This morning, I had the urge to hear the song 'My God' by Jethro Tull. Fired up this online music website, searched for the song, and got a long list of version choices, so I randomly picked one. It wasn't the song I wanted. It was a Jehovah's Witness preacher giving the following sermon…

"An elderly black gentleman and his wife, headed to a Jehovah's Witness meeting deep in the back hills of Alabama, noticed a car following them. Being black folks in the unforgiving South, they were nervous—even downright scared. Following their directions, they turned down a dirt road, driving through a field toward their destination. The car turned, too.

"Now they were certain they were being followed. Unwilling to drive in fear, the gentleman stopped their car and prepared to take action. He rolled up the windows, pressed the locks, and instructed his wife to stay in the car '…no matter what.'

"When he turned to get out, he was startled by someone standing right by the door, holding something in his hands. The gentleman bravely rolled down his window and said, 'What can I do for you?'

"'You Jehovah's Witnesses?'

"'Uh-huh,' said the black man, braced for anything.

"'I've been trying to catch up with you for miles!' the man said, beaming with LOVE. 'My mama wanted to be sure you're well fed after your long drive!' The stranger handed him a pot of home-cooked greens and a pan of macaroni and cheese.

"The preacher paused.

"'Do you see how these people were running from good? I'm here to tell you, my congregation, that many of you are doing the same thing—running away from the good that's trying to catch you. Please, my friends. Slow down and receive.'"

"Wow!" Rishi says. "Good message!"

"Does this mean you're in, Nanette?" Chip asks, not missing a beat.

"I'm in," Rishi answers. "I don't know what I'm in for, but this is certainly most intriguing situation I've been in for a while—perhaps ever."

"I've just got more questions," I maintain, as if there's any chance I'm saying no.

"Ask away." He gets comfortable, crossing his legs in lotus position.

I open my mouth with 10,000 words trying to jump out at once, but no audible sound emerges. Suddenly, I'm so overwhelmed at the prospect of knowing—really knowing—that I can't speak. I look at Chip, dumbfounded.

"Is it okay if I just lay it out for you?" he asks.

My heart's speed beating while my head nods with no help from me. "Okay, I'm ready." I snuggle up next to Rishi. "You?" She nods.

"Here goes," Chip says, legs crossed, straightening up, and relaxing into a classic *mudra*,[35] his thumb pressed against his index finger. "The first, most important thing for you to know in your new role as Earth Ambassador and Publicist for the celestial realms, is what G.O.D. is and what God isn't."

"You mean who, don't you? Should I take notes?"

"No—simply listen. Rishi, please write down the things Nanette needs to study. She'll need your help and support."

The always-ready-to-help soul sister pulls out a notebook and pen, eager to begin.

Oh my God...I have a scribe! I think. I always wanted a scribe. Also a saxophone player to follow me around so my life would have a haunting soundtrack.

"Life on Earth was meant to be decidedly different from how it's unfolded," Chip launches in. "I know this isn't news to either one of you, but the truth is even more fantastic than you suspect. Due to your built-in unrelenting desire to know, you're savvy enough to learn, hold, and transmit it. Just keep remembering that while most things aren't what they appear to be, the good news is that identifying Field Prompts becomes easier with practice." He unfolds his legs and stands up.

"When you follow Field Prompts, you're InFlow. And when you're InFlow, you can readily distinguish Field Prompts. It's a meeting...in a sense."

"Huh?" My head cocks like a dog who just heard a high-pitched noise. "Please go on."

---

[35] Symbolic hand gestures.

"Souls, you know, are not left solely to their own devices on Earth."

"Nice pun-work there," I say.

He smiles. "When you're InFlow, you're following the path of least resistance."

"Okay…"

"G.O.D. is not what most humans believe. The G.O.D. is a more accurate statement."

"Hello! You're preaching to the choir." My hands come together in prayer position, at my heart, and I sing the word, "Hallelujah."

"We're hiring you to help wake up people to the truth of The Field they live in." A dove lands on an outside branch visible through an open window. Its coo catches everyone's attention.

"Briefly, it all has to do with a bet between Lord/SpirIT and Cretin/Lucifer, the prize being ultimate stewardship of Earth for the next thousand years. By the way, Nanette, it's already been written that you take the job, so my advice is to simply accept the overstanding. This is your vocation on Earth. You'll be taken care of as long as you live your mission and exhibit trust."

"Written by whom? Taken care of? Wait a minute… You mean I can quit my job, close down my personal chef business, and all I have to do is promote this G.O.D. you speak of? Is that what you're telling me?"

"Well, I see I found out how to get your attention!" Chip rings a bell from the table next to him. "But not so fast. How's cooking for the priests?"

"As with everything in life, it seems, I have a love/hate relationship with it, depending on which minute of what day— Wait a minute. How'd you know about that?"

"Nanette, I'm not joking. I know whatever I need to know about you whenever I need to know it. Call it a direct line."

"I'm starting to believe you."

"But all I have is access to circumstances, not your innermost feelings. That's where talking comes in. I mean, I've got inklings, but you have nuances."

I lift my shoulders to my ears, contract my body, and blush a little. "That's poetry." I'm getting more and more enamored with the son of Lord with every passing moment. I see Rishi swooning, too.

"Anyway, continue telling me about your job," Chip says.

"Okay. So, the job with the priests? Best part-time cooking job a chef could ever have. It gives me the holy *cuarto*!"

"The holy *cuatro*?"

Rishi, knowing the story, laughs. "You're going to love this!"

I nod. "The first summer I cooked for the Tertians,[36] who were staying at the novitiate for their annual silent retreat, I was tickled with what I thought was an original idea—making a Father's Day cake for thirty priests! When I told Father Murphy, he jokingly rolled his eyes and said, 'I don't know why people think that's so funny...'

"Anyway, it got me thinking. My job gives me fathers and sons. Priests are everywhere, and many of the young men entering the religious order have never been away from home before. They're young enough to be my sons and I'm cooking for them, providing nourishment from the Earth. My job gives me Holy Spirit; it's the Society of Jesus, for

---

[36] Priests in their final formation period in The Society of Jesus.

Christ's sake! And last but not least, my job gives me health insurance. Father, Son, Holy Spirit, Health Insurance…the holy *cuarto*!"

Chip laughs.

"Also, I give them a list and they do all the shopping. They love the food. They're appreciative. The group changes every year, so they never get bored. Oh, yeah, I also get vacation, sick days, and holidays off, and I only work twenty hours a week."

"Come on, Nanette Kenyon," Chip says. "From what I understand, that's unheard of in your world. You must feel fortunate."

"The part that bugs me is having to be somewhere five days a week; I can't travel, I'm not free. I'm stuck in the framework.[37] Ugh. It's so upsetting…I need to rise above."

"Oh, yes…the framework." He leans against me and squeezes my opposite shoulder.

"I meet fascinating people there—priests from all over the world."

"You know," Chip says thoughtfully, "it's no mistake that you work at the Society of Jesus. Lord has been keeping his eye on you for longer than you could ever know."

"Yes, but he's the Lord… Couldn't he keep his eye on me anywhere?"

"He is not 'the' Lord, he's a Lord. One in this Galactic Order."

"Getting nitpicky, aren't you?" I say with a bit a twinkle.

"No! These are important distinctions."

"I ask again, can't he see me everywhere?"

"Aren't you the one who stood in your kitchen four and a half years ago talking to whoever was listening? 'I just

---

[37] E.G.O.'s structure for living.

want a full pantry so I can cook anything I want to cook anytime,' etc., etc."

"Sure did. I keep thinking I should have been more specific—including the sentiments MY pantry in MY house with MY friends eating the food. I guess this is the next best thing. But it just makes my point about being on Earth: getting what you think you want doesn't necessarily lead to contentedness."

The corners of my mouth droop and I let out a big sigh. "I don't know if contentment is even possible. And I've lived a pretty exciting life by most standards." I whirl my finger and wrist around in a whoop-de-do fashion. "Makes me want to not play. Makes me want to leave the planet. Makes me wonder what the fucking point is." My gaze lowers toward the floor.

"I can see you're distraught, Nanette."

"Beyond distraught," I say, beyond distraught.

"There's much for you to learn about the tools available for use by earthlings. And how they're received by humans."

"Finally! This is what I've been waiting for. I've always felt that if I had the right thought in an auspicious moment at the perfect place, or if the stars were suddenly aligned... I don't know—something, anything! Then the true workings of the Earth plane could be known. I guess like it was shown to Buddha. Or Jesus, or Moses. It seems they knew something. And they knew it innately as a true knowing—they couldn't not know it. Whatever it is, once they received it, it was a part of their being. It was who they are. I've always wanted that.

"I mean, I've got no interest in much of anything that's promoted as important on Earth. Never have. Everything's backward. The planet's trashed instead of respected. Whenever I go to put anything in my mouth—which is every day—I freeze because I've got to worry: Is it organic? Is it GMO-free? What has it eaten? Where was it grown? Who touched it with what bacteria?" My fist hits the table. "Blah, blah, blah. Eating is fundamental! It's not supposed to be this difficult. Nor does it have to be." I sip my lemonade.

"Amen!" Rishi interjects.

"The truth is—and I couldn't be more serious—I don't get it. Tell me, Chip. What thought did I have, what action did I take, what subtlety did I accept that brought me to here?"

I jump up and plie, my arms rounded softly above my head.

"Lord wasn't kidding about you!" he exclaims. "It's clear he's been grooming you. And it's perfect. There are things bigger than you, Sunshine."

"So you're saying it's got nothing to do with me, Chipster?" I smirk at him.

"That's not what I'm saying at all. Nice way to put a negative spin on it, though," he chides. I try to do a ballet spin on my big toe and fall over laughing.

"Keep listening, silly. Once a lesson has been truly understood and the embodiment of that lesson demonstrated, circumstances automatically readjust to set up for the next understanding. Your job with the priests will end as soon as you get there… You're on the right track, and here's a little tip. You have one more demonstration to execute there. Afterward? Well, stay tuned for what unfolds."

"How do I know you're not just baiting me to get me to do what you want?"

"Tell me what you really think!" Chip rolls his eyes. "Lord mentioned your feistiness. He said the load was large."

I stand up. "Well, it's not exactly as if you're asking me to get a few articles published and some people to show up to a nightclub! This is some cosmic-proportion, evolutionary, life-changing shit you want me to peddle."

"Yes it is." His gaze takes in my wall of thrift store artwork. It appears as if he's trying to figure out the eclectic assortment of photos, paintings, and posters. I can see him get drawn into a framed poster by MC Escher called "Three Worlds." "Wow..."

"How could anyone say no to what you're offering and live with themselves?"

"Good question, Sunshine!"

I walk over to the couch and sit down. "I don't even know what you're offering... But I know I have to say yes.

"Okay. Yes, I'm in. Go on."

"You still have to do that final demonstration at your job. Saying yes doesn't get you out of it."

"Aw, c'mon!" I play along. "Please?"

"Sorry. It's all part of the training."

"You're funny... I would've said yes anyway."

"Now you can pay attention in a whole different way...with all your newfound learnings, *capisce?* Remember that attention is the price of knowing."

"Yep. I get it."

"Okay... We were talking about what G.O.D. is and isn't. You may be surprised to learn G.O.D. is a Field, not an entity. It's short for Galactic Order of Demonstration."

"Doesn't surprise me at all," I answer cockily. "I've been contemplating that idea for quite some time."

"Yeah, well... Get over yourself," Chip states truthfully. "You've been spoon-fed concepts by Lord himself for as long as I can remember. You'd better've retained something!"

My face jokingly registers fear then relaxes as my brain scans through life's events leading up to this moment. "It's nice to know I'm not crazy."

"Nobody said that," he says...having way too much fun, if you ask me. I playfully stick out my tongue at him while he laughs.

"Continuing..." A purposeful throat clearing precedes his explanation. "Using G.O.D.'s HOME Law Book as a template, Cretin fashioned a great story and called it the Bible. He conveniently left out the parts that would've given earthlings the teachings: the real workings of The Field. The overstandings and understandings needed to grow into fully mature human beings. Instead, with their self-defined rules—confusingly called 'laws'—E.G.O. created three higher authorities. The holy trinity, so to speak—governments, doctors, and gods—that cover mind, body, and spirit. Because this presentation of reality is so accepted as the way it's supposed to be, souls become puppets, adhering to authority, fossilized in E.G.O.'s ways.

"The difference between E.G.O.'s rules and G.O.D.'s laws is quite simple. Laws apply to everyone equally. They don't change according to who you know, who you bribe, your position, or your financial status. That's why in our realm, E.G.O.'s laws are known as 'rules.' Laws are universal. Rules can be forgone to the highest bidder."

Rishi and I high-five each other and clasp hands midair. "Rishi, pinch me. Is this really happening?"

"Oh, it gets better." He high-fives both of us at the same time. For a moment, the three of us touch hands and we feel something wonderful coming through his palms. Rishi's face brightens as she and I look at each other in sheer awe.

"Every earthling begins as a human being, attuned to 'HU'—SpirIT's ultimate vibration. Feels good, doesn't it?"

We nod right on cue. "But when they're raised by people who have blindly bought into and are ruled by E.G.O.'s voices of authority, babies grow into pawns themselves. Even though they're hijacked by E.G.O.'s ways at birth, the spell can be broken. Once it is and The Field is recognized, earthlings recapture their human beingness and can achieve much in this body suit. There are no limits to how far a soul can go. It's up to each individual."

"Please say more about differentiating between puppets and humans," Rishi requests.

"A puppet is a potential human being fossilized in an intricate web of misdirection, which is promoted as 'the truth' or 'the way it is' by those with an agenda of control. You often hear statements such as 'It's my job' coming out of their mouths at the same time they're treating you inhumanely.

"When puppets receive and embrace HU, they become human beings. Receiving the sound of HU is one of SpirIT's most direct communications. It's ordained: E.G.O.-aligned puppets can become human beings that are instruments tuned to the whispers of The Field. But they have to be open.

"Human beings are souls who never bought into—or have awakened from—the hypnotic trance of E.G.O. They understand the Earth plane is a responsive Field and consult it for clues and guidance."

He looks at Rishi. "Like you and I meeting on the beach. Neither one of us resisted the natural attraction we had toward each other, and look where we are now."

She nods once while Chip sips his lemonade. "Damn, that's good!" He slurps until it's empty.

"Human beings have honed their listening skills. They champion people over protocol and they know the difference between E.G.O.'s rules and G.O.D.'s universal laws."

A parking ticket blows off the table onto the floor in front of us. I pick it up and wave it in the air. Chip nods and says, "A perfect example of what we're talking about—the parking ticket demonstrates E.G.O.'s rules. The perfectly timed entrance of the ticket is The Field's playful acknowledgement."

As the sun catches a crystal ornament dangling in the window and rainbows whirl around the room, Rishi points outside. "It's beautiful! What are we doing in here?"

"Anyone want a refill?"

"Many souls fluctuate between puppet and human," Chip offers while I grab the jug. "With the power structure E.G.O. has in place, it's almost unavoidable."

"Such a challenge," I say. "It's so exciting to be a part of the wake-up call."

Once the lemonade is poured, we head outside to enjoy a perfect 78-degree day.

After a while, everyone starts getting hungry.

"Where are we going for dinner?" Chip asks me. "Remember, sky's the limit! I'm on an expense account."

"Literally." Rishi briefly lifts her arms toward the sun in reverence. They both wait for me to speak.

"Hmm. We can spend as much as we want? There are pricey restaurants I've never been to that are supposed to be delicious, but there also some amazing restaurants I'd like to go back to."

I start getting overwhelmed, which is something that happens to me when I've got too many choices.

"We could go to Piccolo, or we could to Fogo de Chao, or we could go to that really good sushi place, Nobu...or Matsuhisa. Oh my—so many to pick from! I just can't decide."

"So this is how linear looping shows up on Earth," Chip mumbles. "Not much different than at the Center."

＊＊

Lord streams into Chip's receiver. "Son, use this opportunity to teach Nanette how to demonstrate knowing. First, help her identify that she is stuck in looping, and then give her the tools for demonstration. This is perfect."

"That's why I didn't let her cook dinner!" Chip beams and his father is quite proud of his alertness on this one. "I knew it'd be a great teaching opportunity."

"Good job. It just took you a few minutes to get your Earth legs. I knew you would. Careful not to get too happy with yourself."

Lord wants to keep him in check as his son gets back to Nanette.

＊＊

"Does it have to be in Los Angeles?" I ask. "Can we go to another city?" I look at Rishi, considering. "Maybe—"

"Nanette!" I'm oblivious. "Nanette!" Chip yells this time.

"What? Why are you yelling at me?" I'm shocked out of my loop.

"Because you didn't hear me the first time! You're snarled up in something we at the Center call 'linear loop-ing.' It happens to the best of us...even Lord. It's okay to tell you that because now you're part of the inner circle."

"Lord has a problem with linear looping?" I ask. "What exactly is it?"

"It's when you get trapped in a thought process and keep going round and round within those thoughts, unable to make a decision or stop long enough to realize you're stuck."

"He gets bottled up like that?"

"It's rare, but when Lord gets really flustered, it happens."

"What could possibly get him all hot and bothered?"

"Have you noticed all the crazy weather?" Chip says. "That's usually a good sign."

"How cliché," I say. "God is mad. Ooh! Thunder and lightning…"

"Not G.O.D., Lord. And not mad. It takes more than that. I'd say livid… He got snarled up in linear looping when he heard about the Law Book not being distributed and the knowledge withheld. It was a big deal."

Chip tap dances a little and ends with his arms pointing toward me. "I hesitate to ask again, Nanette, but what restaurant—in Los Angeles—would you like to go to?"

"Okay. I can do this."

"For Christ's sake," Rishi says, "this is not the last supper you're ever gonna eat. It's one night. One restaurant. CHOOSE!" She blushes, realizing what she just said in front of whom.

"Yes, please. For Christ's sake, choose." He speaks with an amused-as-hell look on his face. "And we'll talk more about the Last Supper later."

"You're right! Rishi, you're right. It's one night, one dinner. I've got this! Let's go to Piccolo. They have the best watercress salad with fresh hearts of palm. I'm melting just thinking about it."

"Done," Chip says. "Let's go. I'm hungry."

seventeen

We arrive at Piccolo and a valet parks the car. I'm beside myself with unadulterated joy. I love good food and I know we're in for a treat.

The restaurant isn't crowded when we get there and we're seated immediately. "Nice place," Rishi says. "It's so warm and inviting; I love the ambiance."

A big bottle of sparkling water is brought and poured into three glasses as my enthusiasm bubbles over. "I came here once with Justine Maxim. You know me and food. I was completely and eternally smitten with the whole experience."

"That's a beautiful and foreboding mask over the fireplace," Chip says. "The mask of 'The Fool'—which I'm sure you both are aware in the Tarot marks the beginning of a journey. The Field is playing with us—all signs point toward our walking the path of acceptance. This is a real treat."

"Really?" I say. "Doesn't being the son of Lord provide you with opportunities that make this seem quite routine?"

"Not in the least. How could one experience possibly make another experience anything less than it is? This place is pure elegance."

"Hmm. I never thought about it like that. And you mentioned 'The Fool' and 'The Field' playing with us… Everything you say warrants ten thousand questions! I love the Tarot."

"We'll get to them over time. As your understanding and overstanding start to merge, you'll begin receiving answers without even vocalizing the questions. That's one of the gifts of building your relationship with The Field."

Just then, our waiter introduces himself. Handsome, neatly pressed, and genuinely delighted to be of service, Fabio exudes warmth and welcome.

"Wine, anyone?" Chip holds up his water glass and waves his hand over it.

"Haha," I say, speaking to the only person on Earth who can authentically make that joke funny.

"I was just going to ask the same question!" Fabio speaks with the perfect amount of an Italian accent. Rishi and I nod yes to the offer of wine. "You are here for *Cena de Quattro? No?*"

My friends turn their heads toward me. My eyes implore Fabio to explain.

"Ahh, you don't know about tonight's special? *Cena de Quattro...*"

"No," I say. "I'm crazy about this place, and Chip, well... He's an exalted guest."

"Ahh, you're in for a treat," Fabio assures us. "Dinner of the Fours. We've put together wine menus based on the four elements: air, earth, water, and fire." He hands us menus. "You choose the wines. Chef Bobo then prepares your dishes based on your selections."

"A wondrous design," Chip says.

"Pietro, our sommelier, is happy to answer any questions regarding the wines..." Fabio directs our attention to a gentleman in the back as I notice the chef coming toward us out of the corner of my eye.

Dressed in a pressed white chef's coat, Chef Bobo's clean-shaven head adds to his commanding presence. "Welcome to Piccolo," he says. "It's wonderful to have you join us for *Cena de Quattro*. We're not too busy yet, so I thought I'd come over and say hello."

"Thank you, Chef," Chip says. "Any suggestions?"

"Be adventurous." Bobo's eyes sparkle. "I'm sorry, I must go. Again, welcome."

"Lord must've had something to do with orchestrating your fantastic choice," Chip mutters as he raises his glass of water toward Bobo, then us. We toast and sip, surprised to find it tastes like wine.

Bobo retreats as Fabio asks, "Anything else?"

"Oh, yes," Chip answers. "If the watercress salad isn't on any of the menus, please bring us each one of them, too. It's Nanette's favorite."

Fabio nods. "With pleasure."

I love that he remembered. Anticipation is palpable as we choose our wines and settle into the evening. Chip excuses himself to "...wash my hands and feet." Rishi and I have never been more intrigued by a living soul in our lives.

He returns to the table just as Pietro delivers a decanter of our first course libation.

"This beautifully balanced wine begins your intrepid journey through the elements: *acqua, aria, terra, e fuoco*." He smiles warmly. "It's Verdicchio di Matelica 2007, from the Marche region near Central Italy. A selection for the element water," he continues, "this wine accompanies the dish called Riccióla."

I lick my lips. "Just wait until you taste it!"

Pietro pours the wine into small glasses. A fresh, empty glass will accompany each item, as we have lots of food to eat and wine to drink.

Just then, three separate waiters, one for each of us, deliver our appetizer...seared yellowtail tuna dotted with thyme-Sicilian oil, accompanied by mozzarella di bufala, and drizzled with Italian ponzu sauce.

None of us waste any time. Silence engulfs the table as the tender fish melts on our tongues—a good indicator of the incredible feast we're in for.

"Close your eyes as you taste it!" I demonstrate.

"Is it possible you're more into food than me?" Chip closes his eyes; sheer delight crosses his face.

"We'll see. I can't wait to cook for you." My heart beats a little faster. "Or with you!"

He finishes his bite. "Let's talk about The Field."

"I'm loving Field Prompts," I jump in. "They're so much better than controlling things all the time."

"You're learning. Recognizing Field Prompts is one of the most important processes to overstand on this Earth plane. We've received one via the elemental design of this dinner. So the elements will guide the evening's conversation."

"'Overstand...' You must be talking about seeing the big picture." I open my arms. Chip nods.

"Sometimes I can't tell the difference between a Field Prompt and the voices in my head," Rishi remarks. "I'd like some direction about that."

"There are ways, and they will become clearer the more you work with them," he offers. "The Field often communicates with human beings via the elements, as each have their own unique signatures. Why do you suppose we're being directed to begin with them?"

"Along with the directions—north, south, east, and west—they help us understand and navigate this realm," Rishi says. "It's not that they give life, they *are* life. With no air, there's no breath. With no water or no earth, there's no food and no body; with no fire, there's no heat or sun. No air, no water, no earth, no food, no body, no sun...no life. It's really pretty simple. Go ahead and call me a pagan." She glows. "I can take it."

"A high compliment," Chip says. "I'm a pagan, and will always respect and follow nature's cues over man's inventtions. Trust me—nature always has the upper hand."

"You mean you're not Christian?" she asks irreverently.

"Jesus Christ, Rishi," he says. "Haven't you been listening?" We all laugh. "Nanette, any thoughts on the elements?"

"I'd say the elements give us beauty, and demonstrate polarities."

Chip relaxes a little more into his seat. "I love listening to you talk about this. Please, go on."

"Life is fraught with—among other things—built-in dualities: seeming opposites pitted against each other that cause unbearable stress on everything and everybody. Language fosters it. The elements teach us there are spectrums."

"Nice, and..."

"Water can give life or drown a thing; fire can purify or burn; air gives life—or too much of it destroys everything in its path. Earth can give you food or bury you."

"And it's not 'either/or,' is it?" he asks.

"No, it isn't!" I say. "I'm aware of the way language sets up the dualistic thinking and I still get caught in the trap. We're all works in progress!" I take a sip of wine and a bite of fish. It melts in my mouth and I sigh in happiness.

Chip raises his glass again and says, "The elements provide the grist for the work of internal transformation—that and more."

All of us at the table receive an inner feeling of sheer ecstasy.

"Wow," I say. "That last bite sent a shiver through my body. It was almost orgasmic."

"Almost?" Rishi wraps her arms around herself.

"That wasn't the fish. That was the cosmos smiling. If we do our jobs correctly, that feeling is something I recommend getting used to."

"**If** we do our jobs correctly?" I tease. "Remember, there is no try—only do."

"Give a galactic traveler a break!" he playfully whines. "Moving on. Water…" The waiter places our watercress salads in front of us. "…brings us to the mechanics of FLOW, which water demonstrates. As I've mentioned, when one exhibits an overstanding of The Field and an understanding of the Universal laws, they're in InFlow."

"I enjoy thinking of water and how it fills any container with its own shape," Rishi says. "It's a powerful teacher."

"The Field, by the way…" Chip nods at Rishi's words. "…is SpirIT's cosmic bridge for offering every incarnated soul **F**reedom **I**n **E**arth's **L**inear **D**imension.

"FLOW is short for **F**luidity **L**ets **O**rder **W**ork, simply meaning that when you follow Universal law, Galactic Order unfolds and demonstration is acknowledged with synchronicity. Don't worry about remembering the acronyms; they're designed to be useful contemplations for helping you to embody the principles. The definitions are inherent in the words themselves."

"I love them," I say.

"We've talked about how Field Prompts work," Chip continues. "Using what's been given to you is all SpirIT wants. It's the key to unifying the opposing elements within yourself. I've always said, and I will keep saying, that demonstration is the only prayer."

"I've often considered that people should be more concerned when synchronicities aren't occurring than dazzled when they are," I say. "This certainly explains it."

"You've been in training your whole life. SpirIT takes the education of his students over-the-top serious when it comes to wisdom. Much of what we're talking about will seem familiar. You just haven't necessarily had the words to describe the phenomenon you've been privy to, or perhaps even the will, after all the struggles you've had. Demonstration takes awareness and practice..."

"Well, that's right on the nose. The second part, that is. The way I grew up made me pray every night to die in my sleep. Waking up in the morning convinced me prayers don't get answered."

"You didn't demonstrate your wish to die," Rishi says, trying to be funny. Chip winks.

"Touché," I say, laughing. "Anyway, it's my feeling that people spend way too much time giving lip service to their spirituality, rather than demonstrating it. If someone is a generous soul, they don't have to tell you; it's obvious by their actions. Same with alignment with SpirIT. I read today that when some Zen Masters work with individuals, they beat them with a stick or throw them out of a window for no reason at all—during particularly nice moments. It is so confusing to them that it stops their minds and they wake up. With a capital W. No amount of talking will do that!"

"Yes." Chip grimaces. "I experienced it myself when I was in training, during my lifetime as Jesus. It certainly stopped my mind."

"I laughed out loud when I read it," I say. "Hey, wait a minute. You had to study when you were Jesus? Why would the son of God need to be schooled? Didn't you arrive already knowing everything you needed to know?"

"I'm the son of Lord, not the son of God. Remember, G.O.D. is a Field, not an entity. You just said it yourself, Nanette: People often give lip service to principles rather than demonstrating them with their actions...or inactions. The Galactic Order of Demonstration is all about *demonstrating* your overstandings of The Field and your understandings of the Universal laws. *Demonstration is the only prayer.* And to answer your question, I trained with master shamans and alchemists from an early age, in many disciplines. Being Son of Lord gave me interest and access, but I still had to do the work, as everyone does. Unfortunately, there are no shortcuts. Fortunately, besides having a direct connection to the authentic Powers That Be, I've retained all the knowledge I've received over many lifetimes and can access it at will. Is retaining your learnings over lifetimes something that appeals to you?"

My mind is suddenly filled with a picture of four-year-old me, with my fists clenched and frustrated face, trying to accomplish just that.

"Ever since she was little," Rishi says.

"Yeah. When I was about four years old, I remember being dumbfounded at not being able to tap into the wisdom gained in other lifetimes."

"You sure were cute—with your tight little fists and scrunched-up face," Chip says. "You haven't changed that much!"

"Thanks... I think. I don't feel that different, either. I still want access. Hey! How do you know what I looked like?" Then I remember he's got his thumb of the pulse of my world—perhaps THE world. "Okay, okay... I'm not going to ask anymore. I get it. You've got a direct line."

Chip takes a bite of his watercress salad. "You were so right on in choosing this restaurant, Nanette. The thin slice of cheese on the bottom of this salad adds just the right amount of salt to the dish. *Perfecto*! And fresh hearts of palm! I haven't had those since the last time Mary cooked me supper. Absolutely exquisite." Chip seems taken back to the experience, "Ahh, Mary."

Rishi and I nod our heads in solidarity as Pietro approaches the table with a carafe of Fiano di Avellino. "This wine accompanies your next dish," he explains. "This grape variety dates back more than two thousand years. Notice the different flavor notes as it flows over your tongue… Wine is to your palate as music is to your ears. If you allow it to, it will transform you."

Rishi and I absorb the poetry of it all.

"Oh, my tongue is tickled with anticipation," Chip says. "This isn't the first time this particular type of wine has followed the element of water. In my previous life, me and my cousin and confidant, John ben Zechariah, celebrated with the spirit of this vine after he ceremoniously dunked me in the River Jordan. In your Bible and stories it's called 'being baptized,' but in truth, it's an invitation to embody the principles of water."

Pietro is bewildered. "John the Baptist?"

"It's a long story," I say.

"Centuries," Rishi pipes in.

"This wine has a good story, too," Pietro says, artfully redirecting the conversation. "It is from the Campania region of Italy and was cultivated by Maura Sarno to recapture the passion and great respect her father, Dominic Sarno, had for their land of origin. We serve this wine to you tonight during the earth course because it was created in honor of the land." He pours three glasses.

Timed with precision, our three waiters approach the table delivering the next course, a colorful tribute to the element earth.

"How do you choose the elemental serving order?" Chip asks Fabio as before us are placed short glasses holding an exquisite dish called *Pomodori e Burrata*—beautifully layered heirloom tomato puree, imported burrata cheese, and basil, drizzled with Larino olive oil.

"By flavor," Fabio replies. "We serve the delicate tastes of water first, the savory notes of earth follows. The fresh flavor of air is third, which leads into the bold flavors of fire. Then…dessert!" he says with a flair. "A little sweetness to carry you off into your night. *Buon appetito!*"

"This is so fancy." I clasp my hands together and wiggle in joy.

Rishi takes a deep breath. "It's elegant."

Silence ensues as we slather the toast crisps with the fragrant combination of flavors, and then deliver them to our taste buds. We each take a sip of wine. I feel transported to the vineyard itself.

"I just ascended," Chip says.

"Shh." Rishi puts her finger to her mouth with her eyes closed, visibly savoring the flavors.

Lord's son regains his composure. He calls us out of our flavor-induced trances, speaking both literally and figuratively. "Okay, back to Earth."

"Have we finished with water?" I take a drink of water. "I don't want to miss a thing."

"Trust me, *mío amore*, we'll have plenty of time together. Tonight we nibble on small dishes and small portions of wisdom so as not to overwhelm." His eyes twinkle. "This is not a rush job. Nature takes its time and gets everything done. So do we."

"We're FLOWING through the meal," Rishi says, grinning and puffing out her chest.

"Nice callback, woman!" I always applaud good comedic timing.

"Thank heavens I've got a team with cognitive ability," Chip says, seeming to speak more to someone else than those of us sitting at the table. He turns his head and crooks his neck as if he's listening to something. "Lord just sent a message that comes directly from SpirIT, who wants me to teach you something."

"These accompany earth," Fabio says, depositing a basket of coal-colored rolls.

"I've never seen bread that black," I mention.

"The action for embodying principles on Earth is known as 'GROW/GROWTH.' We offer for contemplation: **G**iving **R**eceptivity **O**pens **W**orlds **T**hrough **H**eterodox.[38] Without growth, nothing happens.

"Earthlings must be receptive to grow, to create, as well as open to so many things: ideas, wisdom, teachings, and people of every ethnicity, gender, size, and sexuality. They must allow themselves to be a canvas for sadness, fun, laughter, grief, and joy to play out in this arena. Ears are made to listen, eyes to see, and souls to LOVE. And when one is open, every world reveals itself: relationships, wonder, and teachings that, without receptivity, would've been missed."

Chip takes a breath, then a sip of water. "Sorry, I'm extremely passionate about this and can get carried away."

"Sounds pretty important. Please continue!"

---

[38] *Heterodox* means contrary to or different from an acknowledged standard, a traditional form, or an established religion. Both orthodox and heterodox developed from the same root, the Greek *doxa*, meaning "opinion." Heterodox combines *doxa* with *heter-*, a combining form meaning "other" or "different"; orthodox pairs *doxa* with *orth-*, meaning "correct" or "straight." Merriam-Webster.com

Rishi agrees.

"Look at nature!" Just then, Fabio comes over and places a beautiful orchid before us. "I noticed this was missing from your table's ambiance. My apologies for the interruption."

In unison, Rishi and I say, "The Field." Chip, with a knowing smile, nods and continues.

"Feminine receives masculine; an egg, sperm; ground takes in seed; plants light and water. Nature is a living demonstration of this principle. Human beings are transceivers—both transmitters and receivers. Life wouldn't exist without both. To grow, a being must give and receive. Any questions?"

"More of a comment. There is an often-bandied-about adage that preaches, 'You get what you give.'"

"There is so much more to it than that," he says.

"I know!" I say. "I've always said that you can only give what you have."

"Which is why it is so important to keep adding to your personal skills toolbox," Chip says. "The more you have, the more you can give."

"Exactly! It seems to me that the message of the element earth is in alignment with how I've viewed this. *Giving receptivity:* it's an exchange. And what a gift for both parties involved—to receive and to be received! I cannot give you love if I cannot find it in myself to give."

"That all depends on your definition," Rishi says.

"Let's not get off topic," Chip says. "We'll explore LOVE a little later. For now, we'll stick to the earth element and receptivity."

"This is brilliant," Rishi says. "The element earth is feminine, receptive. It's inclusive. **G**iving **R**eceptivity **O**pens **W**orlds. What a beautiful contemplation."

"Nanette," Chip says, "our work for the next seven galactic days is to fully activate your relationship with the elements, the directions, and The Field. You must evolve into a fully functioning, walking demonstration of demonstrating."

"A walking demonstration of demonstrating," I say. "I like it. Collars and cuffs match! Walkin' my talk."

"All teaching is by demonstration, whether earthlings realize it or not," Chip continues.

"How long is a galactic day?" Rishi asks.

"Don't worry about that."

"How much time do we have?" I ask.

"Nice try. Nope. Don't worry about it. You'll know everything you need to know when you need to know it. We've got time."

"What's the difference between manifestation and demonstration?" Rishi asks.

"Chasms," Chip says. "As much as the difference between hope and faith. Contemplate that question, Rishi. We'll talk about it later."

"I will," she says. "I look forward to the conversation!"

"I'll say one thing. When masses of earthlings want to change things, do they stage manifestations?"

"No, they don't," she answers. "They stage demonstrations."

Just then, a large bird flies by the window. "Did you see that?" I say to the table. "A blue heron!"

"An important message from SpirIT." Chip takes a moment. With his palms pressed together, fingers aimed toward the stars, he demonstrates reverence. "SpirIT often communicates on this plane through birds, plants, smells, sounds, other humans—"

"—license plates, billboards, found objects," Rishi offers. She's well versed in symbology and is almost speechless. Almost. "Wow, the blue heron... It traverses comfortably between three of the four elements: water, earth, and air. It hunts at twilight, in between day and night. What a beautiful presentation of gracefully moving through different spaces!"

"Ahh, SpirIT," Chip says after a brief silence envelops the table.

"Pennies!" I say. "SpirIT communicates through pennies."

"Huh?" asks Rishi. "Oh, yeah—the wrist."

"No... Funny, I wasn't even thinking about that. I mentioned them because the last time I was in Denver, I went out to breakfast with a friend. She and I often talk about the reciprocal nature of the Universal field and how everything is medicine. On that day, on our way into the restaurant, I took all the pennies out of my wallet and placed them across the steps of an old brick apartment building. I wanted the next person who crossed that threshold to find them and get happy—or at least crack a grin. We forgot about it and went about our day.

"When we got back to her house, pennies started magically showing up in the weirdest places! Stuck to bottoms of cups, under her son's butt on the bed... When stuff like that happens, all you can do is acknowledge the great mystery. And now I can add the story about my wrist. Pennies *are* magic. Haha!"

Pietro approaches. "We move to reds with our next wine. This beautiful eggplant-colored offering, known as Lacrima di Morro d'Alba 'Rubbjano,' also comes to us from the Marche region of Italy and offers an exotic flavor combination. Please enjoy." He pours.

Waiters appear and Fabio announces, "I present the second offering of earth." Bowls of beautiful *tortelli*—roasted, beet-filled ravioli with parmesan-poppy seeds and brown butter-sage sauce—are placed before us.

"*Gratzie,*" we all say in unison, raising our forks to take the first bite. Again, silence fills the table as we pay reverence to the flavors unfolding on our tongues.

"Beets," Chips says, savoring the flavor of earth. "The color of blood. A beautiful offering representing the earth element. Root vegetables to ground the soul."

"We were talking about receptivity," Rishi says.

"Ahh, yes, we were. Without receptivity, there would be no reception." Chip laughs. "Let's drink and receive this splendid bounty."

We finish the element earth in silence, complete satiation beaming from our faces. Demonstrating receiving in this case turns out to be quite delicious.

Pietro arrives once again at the table holding a decanter of a deep-garnet-colored liquid heralding the forthcoming element, air. "I bring you a unique offering of an ancient grape from the South Tyrol area of Northern Italy," he says. "Legrein Porphyr Riserva; a beautiful wine. Its name reflects the region's purple-red volcanic rock, aptly named as the mineral elements suffuse with rich plums and blackberries. Chef Bobo has created a perfect mate for this wine and element."

Following Pietro, the food arrives, a gorgeous *fagiano*—pan-seared pheasant breast rolled with a smoked, cured prosciutto called "speck" and served with caramelized pears and white port sauce.

"Take a deep breath and welcome air." Pietro inhales the aroma and exhales pure, unadulterated contentment.

We join him in revering the sweet and savory scent as the next course begins; with the first bite, our eyes roll back in our heads at the depth of flavors. Instinctively, all together, our wine glasses approach our lips. We moan in unison.

"Chef Bobo has made my palate happier than it's been in centuries," Chip says.

"It boggles my mind you can say that and not be exaggerating."

"This is an extraordinary night, with stellar human beings."

Rishi, who has a little crush on him, blushes. "He called us human beings, Rishi," I say. "A huge compliment from the son of Lord."

"Don't get up on your high horses just yet," Chip pokes at us. "You still have work to do. The paradox is that you've arrived somewhere, but there is always another 'there' to move toward."

"Free but not free. We're always free to make the next ordered[39] move, right?"

"The next ordered move. Nice." A waiter walks by carrying a cake in the shape of a chessboard with each piece, from pawn to king, shining with fire. "Happy Birthday to You" respectfully fills the air.

"Chess pieces... Nice move, Field!" Chip amuses himself.

"Ordered moves, just like the octave," I say. "The eighth note is the same as the first, only at a higher interval: do re mi fa so la ti *do*. Reminds me of when issues reoccur that I thought I had resolved. The reoccurrence gives me the opportunity to respond differently, from my resolved state and new reference point. To demonstrate a shift in my

---

[39] As in succession, not as in told what to do or commanded to do.

consciousness. To come at the same issue from a new level, demonstrating to myself and The Field how much I've grown. And we know growth comes from being receptive to new ideas, things, and ways of being. Here's to ordered moves."

We raise our glasses in sheer revelry of the night, the company, the teachings, and the learning.

"Air," Chip says. "Too little of it results in no life, and too much brings chaos and destruction to everything in its path. Wind can also be your ally, helping to clear out cobwebs and energies that no longer serve you."

"I love watching the wind," I say.

"Wind gives trees the ability to dance." Arms briefly waving in the air, he demonstrates. "Animating the tension between firmness and flexibility, giving the planted Earth beings motion. Air and water each teach fluidity and flexibility in their own ways."

"Beautiful teaching," Rishi says.

"Without wind, there would be no pollination, and therefore, no growth," Chip continues. "No waves—ocean, sound…no amber waves of grain." A waiter walks by holding a cupcake with an American flag sticking out of it.

"Okay, this getting ridiculous." I laugh. "Really, Field?"

"Wow," Rishi says. "Life here really is magical."

"Wind moves the waves, and carries the whispers that pollinate humanity through Field Prompts. They're often subtle, and require tuning your listening and being receptive in order to learn, grow, and demonstrate acceptance.

"This is a lot to take in," Rishi says.

"Whispers," Chip continues. "It requires astute listening to hear nuances in a whisper."

"Sounds to me as if Father Sky teaches flexibility with the help of wind, and Mother Earth teaches flexibility with the help of water. That's some good contemplation fodder for the fire," I say.

Just then, a piece of flash paper is ignited as Pietro arrives. "And now...fire!"

"I love The Field."

"Good recognition," Chip says.

Rishi, who is in a bit of a spiritual-induced daze, says, "Huh? Recognition of what?"

Chip explains. "Nanette invoked fire and Pietro brought it! Nanette acknowledged The Field. The Field loves to play, starting out with small synchronicities to catch your attention. Once that's achieved, they get larger and larger."

The sommelier continues his informational performance. "I present to you directly from Southern Italy, Tintilia Rutilia d.o.c. 2008, Cantine Salvatore. An aromatic offering. In accompaniment, Chef Bobo has prepared for you one of his favorite dishes, *Animelle*."

A parade of waiters approaches and presents each of us with our plates—elegant works of art that beget an experience of flavor. Fabio describes our meal. "*Animelle* is a crispy sweetbread burger with quail egg, polenta, Portobello chips, and a touch of marsala."

"We'd love another moment with the chef when possible," Chip says to him and he nods with a gracious smile.

Even though the food has been beyond amazing, I recoil a bit at the thought of one item. "Sweetbreads?" My nose wrinkles.

"If you're going to try them anywhere," Lord's son says encouragingly, "this surely is the place. They're one of my favorite dishes—when made with passion. And these are prepared with passion and ability."

Chip's been eating glands for longer than anyone I'll ever know. I take a sip of wine, close my eyes, and bite. Life is good.

***

After a brief reprieve, dessert arrives: a delectable sampling of assorted small bites picked expressly for us by Bobo himself.

"Fabio, how do you say 'extremely satisfied' in Italian?" I ask.

"*Estremamente soddisfatto.*" The words roll off his tongue.

"It had to sound more romantic than English... Bobo!" I say just loud enough for him to hear me in the restaurant's open kitchen. "*Estremamente soddisfatto!*"

He cracks his beautiful smile.

Chip nods to Fabio to bring the check.

He pays the bill in cash, giving Fabio a tip of several thousand dollars as we nod to the staff in appreciation. "Money is truly no object." Chip gives me a $100 bill for the valet.

eighteen

I hand over the parking stub and we wait for the valet to get our car.

"Nanette," Chip asks, "what have been your biggest challenges in life? The most difficult things for you to accept?"

"Well, you, for one. I mean, come on. Lord sent you to Earth to hire me to be the publicist for G.O.D., who's not an entity but a way of life?"

He raises his eyebrows and shrugs, palms up, all while flashing a flirtatious smile.

"You know, according to society, I've 'lost my mind' before, and everything appeared to me as real as you do."

"Tell me about it."

"I thought you knew everything about me."

"As I've mentioned before, I'm privy to the events of your life, but not necessarily your interpretation of them. I'd like to hear the story straight from you."

The young man pulls up with our Toyota and I slip him the cash. He peeks at the bill and his face brightens. "Wow, thank you, man!" We get in and drive off.

"Okay," I continue. "Here's the short version. I was adopted at birth. When I was eighteen, I met my biological parents, which was my dream come true. My adopted parents were divorced when I was a year old; I never had a close relationship with my adoptive father, and since he was despised by my adoptive mother, my brother and I never heard anything good about him.

"Six months after I met my biological dad Ritchie, he either committed suicide or was murdered. I was beyond devastated. I'd just arrived back in Cleveland, after living in San Diego, and planned on spending time getting to know him. The last time I talked with him was at five thirty in the afternoon on the day I got home, and he sounded really strange… He said he couldn't talk. I asked him if someone was there and he said yes. I asked him if it was his girlfriend. 'Yes.' Then he said he had to talk to me later and asked, 'Will that do?' When I said no, he said, 'It's going to have to.'"

We stop at a red light. I take a deep breath. A group of young LA hipsters saunter across the street in front of us. They flash us the peace sign.

"Two days later, my birth mother, Barbara, came to my house early in the morning, sat me down on the bed, and told me he was dead. He'd been found in his home two hours after our phone call. Something inside me already knew. The funeral was an hour after I found out, so I showered and got ready.

"In the shower, I felt the devastation of the news start to close me down. I heard and saw my solar plexus slam shut— I can still hear the sound today. The noise was like the last bit of water going down a drain, and the visual in my head was that of a spiral closing. Like a camera shutter, moving at lightning speed."

The light changes green and we turn left.

"After Richie died, I had no support from the closest adults around me… My adoptive mother didn't even believe he was really my father. She thought her ex-husband, my adoptive father, was my biological father—an illusion that had already been well discredited. Meeting my birth father was the most important thing to ever happen in my life. It was all I'd ever wanted, and I was so excited at the possibility of getting to know him. All that was over in an instant."

"Nanette," Chip says," how did he die?"

"Gunshot wound to the head. It was considered a suicide," I say. "But I've always believed he was murdered. And that belief has nothing to do with not wanting to believe he would kill himself after meeting me. My self-esteem was way too low at that time to think anyone would stick around on the planet just because of me."

We accidentally breeze through a stop sign. I scan the area for the police, thankful it's all clear.

"Wait until you hear this part," Rishi says to Chip.

"On Father's Day that year, I was so excited to be able to call the man whose blood runs in my veins to wish him happy Father's Day. He was excited to get the call, too. But he did something I didn't understand. He put his friend on the phone and made a verbal will: 'If anything happens to me, I want my things to go to Nanette.'

"There are other things that I don't want to go into right now, and in my mind, they all point to murder, not suicide. No matter how much I tried to talk to anyone about it, no one would listen. Since my adoptive mother didn't believe he was my biological father, she wouldn't validate my devastation. She had way too much invested in her 'my ex did me wrong' story to believe the truth. She finally came around, but not for thirty more years. That's another story.

"I didn't handle it well. I spent my days smoking pot, snorting coke, and doing Quaaludes. I contracted hepatitis C from sharing a straw, resulting in six weeks in bed. A few months later, I went back to San Diego and moved in with some friends.

"That's when I started losing it. The whole incident was more than my body, mind, and spirit could take. I started hallucinating. The television and radio were talking to me and everything was a sign. From what my roommates could tell, I needed professional help, so they called the police.

"The officers told them they couldn't take me unless I was a threat to myself or others. My friends suggested they come and talk to me for five minutes. Within three minutes, I was in the back of the squad car.

"At the bin, as I like to call it, I was told that I'd taken too much acid—which wasn't true. That I was schizophrenic—which wasn't true. That if I ever smoked pot again, I would do irreversible psychological damage and most likely live out my life in an institution—also not true. They drugged me and asked me endless, useless, stupid questions, none of which helped me. None of these 'professionals' had any idea what I needed. I was in shock and traumatized. I needed love, not medication."

"The story's so different hearing it directly from you," Chip says.

"Here's the part I wanted to tell you. When Ritchie died, I couldn't believe it. My life up until that point had been so difficult, with almost every grown-up around me using me as a dartboard to relieve their anger and hate at their own circumstances. When I met him, I felt as if I was finally getting a little break. Words don't exist to describe the way I felt when he died.

"To the outside world, I had a nervous breakdown. I was so scared and confused.

"When I look back on that part of my life, I feel as if the trauma of that event opened me up to see the way this place really operates. How connected everything is. The matrix… I've seen it. I swear to this day, all the mystical events that happened were as real as you are, but others will tell you different. Which brings me to my point: a) Is this really happening? And b) by stepping into this role you're offering, am I setting myself up to end up in a locked ward again? I'm not so into that."

I grin. "After I got out of the bin, I moved to San Francisco. Walking down Fillmore Street one day, a homeless guy offered me ten cents for a cigarette. I felt as if I were right back on the unit and contemplated the truth behind the idea that Earth is the mental institution of the universe. I mean, it's really no different in or out of the psych wards. Just like one of my favorite movies, *The King of Hearts*, it's difficult to tell the patients from the guards... And who saves the town, anyway? What I mean is, I'm not so sure we're not all really just locked up anyway."

"Here's to you, love. Beautiful questions." Chip reaches across the seat and puts his hand on my shoulder. I tear up.

"You've clearly been tempered for your role," he says, "and to help you fully receive your vocation, we'll sit in ceremony together."

Suddenly, music wafts out from my purse as the song "Madre Ayahuasca" mysteriously starts playing on my phone. "Are we sitting with *La Madre?*"

"Ahh," Chip replies. "The Field acknowledges our listening with synchronicity."

When we arrive at my house, I park and shut off the engine.

Wiggling around uncomfortably in my seat, I can't believe what I'm hearing. People have often said they meet Jesus in a ceremony. How often does one get to sit with him? Oh boy. I hope I'm not delusional.

"We begin *dieta* soon," he says as we get out of the car. "Rishi, I hope you'll be joining us."

"Thank you for the invitation. I would be honored."

"We'll go to Peru and sit with Otorongo."

"Otorongo?" I'm quite astonished. He's a master shaman, well respected among his peers and in the Shipibo nation. "I've drunk with him before, experiencing some of the most powerful ceremonies I've ever participated in. Do you know what '*otorongo*' means?"

Chip offers each of us a mint before he and Rishi head down the driveway. "You'll begin to see more and more connections between your past, the present, and the future, without having to 'lose your mind,' Nanette. Your life has been one big education, and now it's time for you to assimilate and teach the message. Oh, yes…'jaguar.'"

nineteen

The next morning, Chip arrives at my house and lets himself in with the key I provided. He finds me in the kitchen.

"You're just in time for breakfast! Coffee? Bacon? Eggs?"

"Yes. Yes. Yes," he replies. "But lighten up on eating for the rest of the day. We begin *dieta* tomorrow."

"Tomorrow?"

"Our plans have changed," he announces. "Otorongo's coming here instead of us traveling to him. We must prepare to receive him. Where shall we journey together?"

"I'll ask Rishi to call the ranch in Topanga. Or maybe Ojai is a better idea... I don't know. Give me until the end of the day. When should we reserve it for?"

"Ojai is better. We'll leave tomorrow and spend three days in preparation. I'm going to teach you and Rishi how to enter ceremony. You see, your approach sets the tone. It's so much more important than people give credit."

"You know, Chip. I've got things to do over the next few days. I can't just drop everything!"

"Get out of your commitments. Tomorrow's the first day of training, and there will be no distractions."

"Okay, your Highness," I say with a great deal of exaggerated indignance. "I'll just tell my boss that I'm working for G.O.D. now. The Jesuits should understand that. They probably think I'm working for God already!"

Chip laughs.

"You're going to be just fine, Nanette. Don't worry about feeding the priests. They'll be replacing you soon enough."

twenty

It's just after two a.m. and the sky's only lit by the sliver of a new moon. Board members begin arriving at The Grove while Cretin peruses the grounds, extremely impressed with Larry's keen attention to detail. Everything he instructed him to do is set in place, and the elements he took upon himself to add are tasteful and limited, showing just the right amount of initiative.

Larry calls from the hotel, checking in before supposedly leaving for the airport.

"I'm impressed with your efforts. Spend an extra night in the hotel and enjoy the area. Take yourself out to dinner. It's all on the company."

"Thank you! How generous."

"You're welcome. And you're on call. Keep your cell phone on."

Cretin retires to his suite to prepare for the morning's events as The Grove awakens. The ancient trees always welcome their guests.

As each Board member arrives, they're met by their own personal valet, gin fizz in hand, and guided to their weekend's retreat suite. A private, stocked-to-personal-preference den of inequity. Pampered? Spoiled? Entitled? These words don't begin to describe the excess and indulgences these men are accustomed to.

***

SpirIT summons Lord to The Grove to witness the grandeur of E.G.O.'s cabal.

"Here's what you're up against. Cretin's a master alchemist who, in an effort to gain control, power, and admiration, learned the secrets of The Galactic Order. Feeling quite enamored with his accomplishments, he began using his newfound tools to enact revenge on anyone in his past who did him wrong, and put to death any other alchemists who had uncovered the true work-ings of The Field, nature, and transformation. He found other wretched souls who took well to being followers and... Well, you know the rest of the story."

"The way I understand it," Lord answers, "The Field, inherently impartial, cultivates expansion in accordance with the internal direction of the user. E.G.O. bent the laws of demonstration, altering the meaning of key words and wrapping mortals in a story so grand, so suppressive, and so accepted that the true laws of Mother Earth are nowhere on their radar screens. Sadly, most of them have no clue. All the while E.G.O. promotes the idea that evil is some form of divine punishment for sinning and that some creature called 'the Devil' is responsible for it all."

"You have quickly assimilated all the new infor-mation you just received," SpirIT acknowledges. "Remember, they will always seek to control the order of things and vilify nature in their quest for unlimited power. Cretin has a beef with you, too, which fuels the fire."

"I just finished delivering this teaching to the team," Lord says. "Cretin and I have had issues for a long time."

"Well done. You have the right attitude, my sweet Lord," SpirIT says. "I really want to see you earn your eternal advancement on this one. I feel it coming."

SpirIT points a finger toward an orchestra and George Harrison, singing "My Sweet Lord," pipes in.

***

It's just after five a.m. and the ceremony space glows with ominous electric blue light. Ultramarine tones dapple across the lake and glimmering shadows dance on the trees. The Great Owl glows officiously, welcoming back the masterminds of E.G.O.'s reign.

As a masked ferryman on the opposite side of the lake prepares Dull Care's[40] effigy and positions his boat for launch, attendees robed in brown hooded cloaks begin to move toward their seats.

Larry's just about to cut through the back way onto Grove property when his cell phone blasts Cretin's personal ringtone—the theme from *The Godfather.* "Shit!" He lowers the sound as he answers, "Good morning, Cretin."

"Pick up Lakshmi from the Sonoma County Airport. Be sure she's here and ready to read by nine thirty."

"Righto." Larry's shoulders drop and he lets out a deep sigh. He turns around and heads back to the car. Suddenly, his focus changes. In one sweet instant, he realizes, *I get to spend time with Lakshmi!* The consolation prize could almost be as good as the original plan.

***

The clock strikes six. A procession of priests wearing hooded robes colored bright red, blue, and orange— reminiscent of a colorful Ku Klux Klan rally—enters from the trees, collectively carrying a pyre-shaped altar in one hand and a stick of fire in the other. When the group arrives at the shore, they position the crematorium and extinguish their torches.

---

[40] Bohemian Club members claim the definition of "Dull Care" is worry. Conspiracy theorists conjecture it means "compassion" or "conscience." "Dull Care: Origin, Usages and Meanings," Daurade, Illuminati Mind Control website.

At the base of the Owl, priests and "tree spirits" ritualistically dance and sing songs recognizing Dull Care. Quite the spectacle: The high priest is in a pink-and-green satin costume; next to him, a tree spirit prances in a gold spangled bodysuit dripping in rhinestones. Together, they frolic as they chant songs honoring the division in a man's heart between "reality" and "fantasy," and of how vital it is to escape to a world of fellowship among men. Vaguely homosexual undertones abound, which is common at The Grove. Among themselves, the men enjoy intimate acts behind closed doors, but feign offense and legislate against same-sex relations in public and political forums. The dance ends with the group of them in a suggestive embrace.

A gong clangs.

The ceremony[41] begins. Dull Care embarks on its journey toward death. The ferryman, dressed in a black hooded robe, appears in a puff of smoke on a black gondola ornamented with carved human skulls. He slowly poles the vessel toward the pyre…

The high priest speaks:

The Owl is in His leafy temple;
let all within The Grove be reverent before Him.
Lift up your heads, oh ye trees,
and be lifted up, ye everlasting spires…for behold!
Here is Bohemia's shrine,
and holy are the pillars of this house.

The gong clangs again.

---

[41] The ceremony has been edited for artistic purposes. Information is available on the web if you wish to research The Bohemian Club.

Hail Bohemians!
With the ripples of waters,
and the song of birds,
such music inspires the sinking soul,
do we invite you into Springtime's joy.
The sky above is blue and sown with stars.
The forest floor is heaped with fragrant grit.
The morning's cool kiss is yours.
The campfires glow...
The birth of rosy-fingered dawn.
Shake off your sorrows with the city's dust
and cast to the winds the cares of life.
Our pyre awaits the corpse of Care...

The funeral march begins as the ferryman, his face
painted like a skull, gets closer to his destination.

Oh Thou, thus ferried across the shadowy tide
In all the ancient majesty of death...
Dull Care, ardent enemy of beauty
Not for Thee the tender forgiveness
or the restful grave.
Fire shall have its will of Thee
and all the winds make merry with Thy dust!
Bring fire!

The Owl continues:

Be gone detested Care! Be gone!
Once more, we banish Thee!
Be gone, Dull Care!
Fire shall have its will of Thee!

> Be gone, Dull Care and all the winds
> make merry with Thy dust!
> Hail this Lamp of Fellowship's eternal flame.
> Once again, this spring equinox sets us free.

With that, Dull Care is torched as the men explode in a chorus of cheers, applause, and "huzzahs."

Just then, the Master of Ceremonies appears on the stage in a puff of smoke, as if magically coming directly from the vapors.

"Take ye all a goblet of wine and hold it toward the starry sky as we acknowledge our great source of power."

The men hold their glasses toward the day-breaking sky, a new moon barely visible beside the just-risen sun.

> "Wine brings light to the hidden secrets of the soul,
> gives being to our hopes,
> bids the cowards flight,
> drives Dull Care away,
> and teaches new means
> for the accomplishment of our wishes."

The MC holds up his glass to the crowd. A toast ensues with reverberations of Baccarat crystal. The soul-moving resonance cleans away any stagnant energy and clears space for the new.

"A few announcements," he offers. "We reconvene at nine fifteen sharp to prepare to meet with Lakshmi at nine thirty. Lakeside Chats begin after lunch and go all day. Mandatory attendance, gentlemen—I almost forgot, and ladies—it's why we're here. Dress well, revered Board Members; we broadcast to the conference directly after the reading. Meeting adjourned."

twenty-one

Larry has his usual breakfast at a local diner—bacon, eggs, hash browns, rye toast, and English Breakfast tea—then heads to the airport to pick up the Oracle. On the way, he breathes in the beauty of Sonoma County's rolling hills, blue skies, and scattered vineyards. A red-tailed hawk flies along beside him, gliding on the wind flows, and then vanishes into the distance.

He arrives at the airport just in time to see Lakshmi emerge from a set of automatic doors. Larry leaps out of the car and introduces himself. After opening the passenger door for her, he puts her two totes in the trunk, climbs in the car, and off they go.

Surprisingly uncomfortable, Larry fumbles for words. He's never been around an Oracle before.

"How was your flight?" He signals and changes lanes.

"Is that what you want to ask me?" She tilts her head and gazes toward him out of the corner of her eye.

"Uh, no... Well, yes. I care about how your flight was..."

"It was fine."

"Okay, yes, I do have questions. Can I ask you 'oracle things'?"

"You mean you want to know about your future?" Larry cracks a smile.

"All I can tell you is this... Things are about to get very different, and you are a part of the change. Watch for signs."

She waves her hand. With a gentle smile, she's finished with the conversation.

twenty-two

Cretin and the Board are all in their seats ready for the reading to begin. Lakshmi's ready, too, dressed in long white flowing robes with hair so black and shiny it resembles a raven's wing. She's a sight to behold as she walks barefoot toward the stage, the bottoms of her feet receiving the vibrant energy of the forest's lush ground. Her ankle bracelet is the only audible sound, aside from the deep rumblings of living redwood trees.

Cretin joins Lakshmi and leads her by the hand toward a fan-backed chair located center stage. She's flanked on either side by her amulets, talismans, and other power objects, including crystals, feathers, tobacco, sage, wooden "strike anywhere" matches, and a stack of books. Her deck, wrapped in silk, sits on top of a bamboo table. Canned thunder booms. Staged lightning completes her mystical appeal.

Lakshmi begins the ceremony by creating her sacred space. She strikes a match off the floor, lights the tobacco, and blows it in the seven directions, saying a little prayer with each one. She calls in, welcomes, and thanks the ancestors, elementals, and her personal guides.

"The question is how to proceed, taking into account recent events in the house of G.O.D., correct?"

"Yes, Lakshmi, that's the question," Cretin responds. "We're ready to begin."

Lakshmi shuffles the deck as she peruses the crowd. She stands in silence, commanding the space, refusing to speak until they're settled and focused.

"You didn't bring me here to tell you fairy tales," Lakshmi begins. "I say what I see regardless of whether you find the message palatable. In other words…" Lakshmi lowers herself down on one knee with her arms open before her. "Please don't shoot the messenger."

She's not kidding and smiles nervously.

"Begin," Cretin commands.

Lakshmi rises and sits down. She pulls the table toward her and shuffles the deck. "We're using the Celtic Cross Spread today, observing and considering the situation from every angle."

She lays out the cards as a cold wind touches her neck. Flipping one, she says, "The first card speaks to the heart of the matter—Six of Swords—lives in transition. Auspicious or ominous? The Six of Swords reminds us that in order to move forward, the past must be left behind.

"Gain perspective by viewing the situation as a whole. Meaning, before moving forward, you must identify the wounded parts of yourself—and E.G.O. as an organization—and heal them. I'm being guided to read you a passage from The Mythic Tarot regarding this card."

Lakshmi pulls the book from the stack next to her and opens it. An object flutters to the ground. She picks it up and stands there, trembling in silence. She gathers her words. "This is a postcard from Auschwitz." She holds it up as chills consume her. "I don't know how it got into this book." A rumble goes through the crowd.

***

SpirIT tunes into Lakshmi, one of IT's favorite Awakened Weavers wandering Earth. "It's important they know their evil methods are visibly present in The Field, Lakshmi," SpirIT imparts. "The postcard is a message for Cretin, who understands the meaning. It's telling him the clandestine ways of the past are now visible."

SpirIT plays a harp and Lakshmi, now balanced, continues.

**

"We've clearly stirred up the dark side of control with this question."

Lakshmi's eyes beam out over an entranced crowd and lock on Cretin, who clearly gets the message. He motions for her to get moving.

"The cards say you must accept the reality of what's at hand. Once you do, a sense of relief will be coupled with knowledge of the serious work ahead. After the relief of acceptance, the realities will reveal themselves."

Lakshmi pauses, brings her hands to her chest, and says a quick prayer. She's spooked, but must remain professional and strong. She flips the next card.

"Here we learn about the forces helping or hindering the situation." She speaks slowly. "Ahh, Three of Cups. Celebrate what you've accomplished... Exactly what you're doing! Join together in revelry; tighten your bonds. Think of Ancient Rome, where men consorted with each other, regardless of sexual preference, simply to strengthen the constitutions of their fight. It's an example of the lengths you may be asked to go to pull this off. You must preserve cohesiveness in order to maintain your strength.

"Next card: Four of Swords, suggesting the best actions to take now. It speaks to the 'calm before the storm' and advises you to unwind and gather your strength so you can move forward well rested. Again, your current actions are in alignment with its message—retreat, rest, and rejuvenate. Refuel your tanks, and while you do, observe Lord as he puts his plan into action."

The group's collective sigh wafts through the trees. Sybil Veda[42] leans over to Janus Kiro.[43] "Same message as *The Art of War*."

"Ahh, Eight of Swords," Lakshmi continues, "showing the hidden factors surrounding the situation. There are serious disturbances on the path. Keep your attention on the goal, being careful to not let yourselves get thrown off course by unexpected obstacles, both internal and external. At some points, it will seem as if any way you move will cause you trouble. Herein lies the lesson: you must let go of the way it's been to move on. There are forces at play you cannot control. More importantly, they will hurt you if you try. This card says you must be knocked off your high horse and assures you it's coming."

Cretin rolls his eyes.

"While this card bespeaks of a great fall or bad fortune, it focuses on the solution, which is, as you move forward, to leave pride behind and ask for help. It might feel as if you lost something, but in truth, when you lose, you win."

"That's some skilled doublespeak," Sybil whispers to Janus. "Better watch out for your job!"

"Again, now it's all in how you move forward.

---

[42] Minister of Education, Formation, & Compliance, Dept. of Misinformation

[43] Minister of Public Affairs & News, Dept. of Misdirection & Spin

"Our next card reveals the effect that brings the past into the present. It's a court card, the King of Swords, representing the person you must go to for the help recommended in the previous card."

As Lakshmi reads, the tenor around the forest floor is awe and amazement. Every card she pulls speaks directly to the situation and is clearly unfolding in a particular, seemingly prescribed order.

"This person is visionary, with key information from the past that will alter the course of the future," she continues. "What you'll notice most about them is their capacity to inspire people and motivate change.

"Any questions?" Lakshmi stops for a drink of water.

"Who is it?" a random voice floats up from the group. Cretin shakes his head, implying Lakshmi should continue without questions.

"Cretin will discuss that with you later," she answers. "This card, revealing your next step, is the Ace of Pentacles.

"It speaks to a renewed energy surrounding the issue, but warns of the pitfalls associated with greed and overconfidence. Again, it suggests seeking proper advice from the King of Swords. If you truly accept the lessons and growth that come with it, this card foretells complete material success."

Lakshmi turns over the next card. For a split second, her face appears to have seen a ghost. A wave of nausea comes over her.

"The Devil card shows how you see yourselves."

A mixture of sighs, exhales, and nervous laughter emanates from the group. Lakshmi pauses and sweeps the space with an eagle feather from her altar before continuing.

"This card, in this position, is a little frightening. Remember, I say it as I see it." The group becomes silent. Even the forest quiets. "You see yourselves as the gatekeepers to both good and evil. You know what you're doing, and you know who you are; you dance to your own tune and see only what you want to see."

Lakshmi looks up to the trees and brings her palms together at her heart.

"This card is telling you it's time to come to terms with the shadowy nature of your presence in the world. There are unexplored parts of yourselves that need to be accepted in order to transform the situation at hand. The power of darkness is at your fingertips, and because of this, you've forgotten the nature of light. A new wave of energy is entering and you have to become new to work with it—and to survive it in any form. Probably not the one you've grown accustomed to."

"Let's move on," Cretin says. "We're on a schedule."

"Okay," Lakshmi says, "but one more thing. This card speaks to the way you control your inner and outer worlds, the darkness and the light. You—presently the keepers of the keys to the structure of society—must search out the things you fear most, and address them, live with them, embrace them. The message I'm being told is, 'Perhaps it's loss of perceived power?'"

"MOVE ON!" Cretin roars. Unable to manage his anger, he briefly starts to shape-shift. His teeth spontaneously sharpen and his skin appears to grow scales. Gil runs over to him and slaps him on the back, awakening him from his rage. He returns to his previous troll-doll-like self.

"Moving on... Prince of Wands is in the position of how others see you. How are you viewed by the world? Well, not so good.

"You're viewed as broadcasting mistruths, unbelievable messages, shallow promises... Opportunistic. People trust you to be who you've proven you are, and that scares them. They know your plan is to take care of you and yours, disregarding everyone else—with an agenda for power and domination instead of compass-sion and peace."

Cretin glares at her. "Next card."

Lakshmi takes in a deep breath and exhales, re-leasing some of the inevitable inner tension that would arise in anyone in this situation. "Your biggest fears. Interesting, because a previous card says you must embrace your fears... So what's important for you to embrace? Ahh, Two of Cups. A reconciliation of a love broken up. Do you understand?"

Lakshmi peruses the crowd, seeing expressions of belief, satisfaction, disbelief, vindication, anger—a rainbow of emotion.

"Continue to the next card, please," Cretin demands. "We understand."

"The outcome card. If you follow the guidance suggested, making the alterations in your thought and actions mentioned in this reading, this card presents what can be accomplished. Consider it 'the carrot.'"

Lakshmi turns it over and a look of relief crosses her face. "Six of Pentacles—success. But again, it depends on making the changes necessary to hold and be held by the new container. Via the planets, these are the specific steps to take: Saturn—follow step-by-step procedures; Jupiter—be open and flexible to options not previously entertained; Venus—success will come when you follow your heart; the Moon—success is attainable if you operate authentically. Mercury—organize your communications so context and timing are aligned; and Mars—consistent energy, rather than sprints or marathons."

Lakshmi stands up and walks around the table toward the front of the stage. "This reading has a consistent theme that is almost being driven home with a hammer. Something somewhere is hoping you get the message."

"Meeting adjourned," Cretin yells, pounding his fist on the arm of his chair.

"One more thing before we close." A shiver runs through Lakshmi while she stands her ground. Cretin allows her to continue.

"The reading began with the Six of Swords. Swords present the element of air and/or mental concepts. The reading ends with the Six of Pentacles. Pentacles present Earth and the physical. As a whole, this reading says something in the air is being brought down to Earth. That's what you're being shown. Please remain seated while I close the ceremony. Thank you."

Lakshmi lights tobacco and blows it in the four directions, above and below. She puts her hands together at her heart and bows her head.

The reverence is too much for Cretin. He abruptly interrupts her closing moment. "Meet in the broadcast room in fifteen minutes. We're live at the conference in thirty."

twenty-three

E.G.O.'s TASTE Conference is well underway with a breakfast spread that inspires awe even to those accustomed to the lifestyles of the elite: lavish bowls dripping with fresh tropical fruits, berries, creams, crepes, meats, egg dishes, herring, smoked fishes, loaves—and everything else you could possibly imagine.

"Start the presentations!" Gil instructs Zephyr from an outdoor office at The Grove. "We've got a lot of ground to cover."

"Okie dokie, Gilbert."

Zephyr messages the announcer to broadcast a warning. Instantly, the lights flash on and off three times and the loudspeaker booms: "All delegates please meet in the main auditorium in ten minutes."

He heads to the stage himself, whizzing past conference attendees on his personal transportation device that's really something to behold. It hovers five inches off the ground and has a platform connected by three poles and topped with a handrail. Access to it is a benefit of his position—one of the many things he'll lose if he chooses to quit or fails to dazzle.

Zephyr straightens his clothes and prepares to meet the crowd. Balloons are released, music swells, and the loudspeaker booms: "Please welcome your host and the executive producer of TASTE, our very own Zephyr!" He strides to center stage as the crowd erupts into a standing ovation.

"Welcome! Sit, sit. We hope you enjoyed breakfast. It's the only meal of real food you're getting this weekend!"

The crowd cheers and laughs, but he isn't laughing. "I'm not kidding," he says. "New information and changes will be revealed. Some you may not like so much."

Zephyr realizes his disdain is showing, so he curbs his reverse enthusiasm. "Thank you! Thank you for all you do, and for your dedication."

The crowd applauds.

"Now is the moment many of you have been waiting for. The world we live in is rapidly changing. Are you ready to meet the men and women who keep us safe and secure? The people behind the scenes who so brilliantly keep this machine running? The wizards behind the curtain, so to speak? Welcome to Oz!"

The crowd at the convention center cheers, applauds, and whistles.

***

At The Grove, Cretin cringes at the Oz reference. It's all he can do not to jump through the camera and strangle him. If looks could kill, Zephyr would have spontaneously combusted. Cretin makes a mental note to speak with Lucifer about Zephyr's disobedience to the Order, albeit a potentially touchy conversation.

***

"This has never happened before, and it will never happen again," Zephyr continues from the convention center stage. "Please hold your applause until the end."

A screen appears behind him, broadcasting a view of the most elite of Elite Global Order's Powers That Be directly from The Grove's state-of-the-art media center to the convention hall's main stage.

"Introducing the man in charge of all your needs all the time, and the forerunner in assuring our role in Global Corporate Citizenship, Board President and CEO of Time/Space, Gil Gamesh."

"Thank you, Zephyr."

Gil leans into the camera and points a finger toward the people. "Together, we can do anything. I'm looking forward to bringing you all up-to-date on the plans we have for your future. I hope you're excited, because I know I am!"

"Thank you, Gil." Zephyr continues, "Now for our Media Department... Janus Kiro, in charge of Public Affairs and News, is right here!"

"Hello, everyone!" She offers a queen's wave. "We strive to keep you informed, in the know, and on top of things: 24 hours a day, 7 days a week, 365 days a year. Thank you for being there!"

The crowd gets caught up in her exuberance and starts to applaud, but only briefly. Then they obediently stop themselves.

"Next, meet the man who ensures you're always entrained—I mean entertained—Minister of Entertainment & Arts, SakuDoka."

Zephyr pats himself on the back, tickled by his "slip."

"Pay no attention to the men and women behind the curtain!" SakuDoka says and bows to the camera.

Zephyr, watching him closely, catches E.G.O.'s Master of Spin giving Cretin a knowing wink before taking his seat in the media room.

"Next up," Zephyr says, "making sure you and yours are properly schooled, meet our Minister of Education, Formation, and Compliance, Sybil Veda." She stands up and points to her head.

"The most important tool you were born with is your brain," Sybil spouts. "It's vital our people keep them sharpened, and I'm here to ensure you've got all the help you need to do that." She goes back to her chair as the next speaker steps before the camera.

"In the spirit of human genome advancement," Zephyr continues, "welcome Gene Edicts, CEO of the Scientific Advisory Committee."

"Thank you, Zephyr. Hello, friends! I want to assure you we'll never stop working closely with the Elite Health Administration to provide you with the medicines you need to stay happy, healthy, and a successful, contributing member of society—in one way or another. Even if it's donating your organs."

Zephyr pauses as the band Blondie holographically appears on stage and Debbie Harry belts out, "One Way Or Another." They fade away.

"And now, meet Leon Pius," Zephyr says, "Minister of the Elite Health Administration."

"Thank you, Zephyr!" Leon holds up a prescription pad. "Don't worry about a thing. We've got something for everyone."

A smattering of clapping comes from the crowd. "Again, please hold your applause," Zephyr reminds them. "Now, introducing the man whose job it is to keep you informed about our planet and its resources, Minister of the Renewable Energy Resource Group, Robert Slick."

"Thank you for continuing to support us in meeting our global energy platform objectives," Robert says. "You've got TASTE!"

The crowd roars. Zephyr glares at them and their enthusiasm reluctantly subsides.

"Perfect time to be introduced to a man who, as Minister of our Environmental Protection Agency, is creating an Earth that works for us—molding the planet and nature to meet man's needs! Please welcome Monty Santo."

"That was quite the introduction, Zephyr," Monty says. "It's true... The planet is here to work for us, not vice versa. I'm here to ensure it will be able to accommodate the Earth's growing population, whatever it takes."

"What would we do without you?" Zephyr says. "Thank you for caring so much." Inside, he cringes before introducing Minister of Religion, Amos Duff.

"Praise God!" Amos bellows as he raises his arms, whipping the crowd into a frenzy. "Can I get a 'Hallelujah!'?"

"Hallelujah!" the crowd echoes back.

"Always remember, God is everywhere...and he's watching!"

Amos tosses holy water toward the camera, blessing the crowd at the convention as the camera at The Grove pans to the puppet master of the free world, Cretin, with Zephyr's voiceover. "And now, please say hello to our Grand Wizard and Master Alchemist, Cretin of E.G.O.! You may applaud."

The crowd goes wild.

"Thank you. You're a good little worker."

171

Zephyr's face turns red as heat rises within his frame. He secretly gives Cretin the finger.

Cretin, sitting in his fan-backed chair on a red velvet dais designed to highlight his power, addresses the crowd from The Grove.

"Give yourselves a round of applause for all of your greatness. You're terrific! As a matter of fact, go ahead and pat each other on the back. You're doing the heavy lifting, and we're so pleased to have your undying support."

Applause breaks out in the room and the delegates all give each other a hearty slap.

Jumping to his feet, Cretin continues. "The world's changing at a rapid pace, and we're all being transformed along with it. This weekend will be unprecedented— we're introducing new policies and programs, we're letting you in on never-before-known E.G.O. practices, and we're re-energizing you to go back to your domains and lead the way. You've got TASTE!"

The crowd erupts in a joyous outburst of self-justification.

"We're at a crossroads. Victory depends on all of us coming together and moving forward in an orderly fashion. Become educated about your assigned position in the order. You should know your job so well that you can perform it in your sleep! The time is now to step into your best self and, as the kids say, 'Bring it!' It's a full-court press."

Cretin, his remarks finished, nods toward the crowd, taking in their adoration, then sits down.

"Now, I'd like to introduce our final Board member, a man who single-handedly—along with a team of brilliant nerds…" Zephyr winks. "…gives us the tools to bridge the virtual world with the physical world. A man whose genius is paralleled by few and who has deigned to visit you in person today, please welcome to the TASTE stage, Will Gateways."

Dancers in sequined leotards, fishnet stockings, and multicolored Vegas-style feathered headdresses kick line in from both sides of the stage as a large clear tank of water rises through the parting floor. Will walks on the water as he comes forth. It's quite the visual. Lights flash, water fountains dance, and the room is filled with elation.

"I'm thrilled and honored to be with you today," Will says. "You've got TASTE!"

Preselected members of the crowd shoot streamers into the air as the convention's theme song swells to a crescendo.

Will has the crowd in the palm of his hand. He just has this way about him.

twenty-four

The dancers high-kick off the stage as Will gets serious.

"I'm going to brief you on the latest technological advances, as well as preview innovations you're going to be very excited about." Will, a big smile on his face, nods his head. "Go ahead!" He claps his hands repeatedly as the crowd cheers and applauds.

"Technology in all areas is advancing faster than you can blink your eyes. The newest systems are obsolete before they even come to market.

"Today we welcome the future: the future of technology, of science; the future of medicine, education; the future of food; and the future of mankind...humankind. We've come a long way. We can sit at our desks and connect with people thousands of miles away in real time. With smartphones, video cameras on every corner, and home entertainment systems that keep us connected, we're safer and more informed than we've ever been.

"We can print body parts on 3-D printers, we can genetically modify seeds for sustainable crops, and we're just now leaving the gate. We still have a long way to go. And we can't do it without you!"

The crowd goes crazy, chanting, "Gateways! Gateways!"

Will continues. "We've been planning this for a long time—'greasing the wheels,' so to speak. Slowly and steadily installing more and more programs that offer greater features for the user while enhancing security,

sustainability, and sanity. Creating a 'norm' designed for us, by us. The more virtual the world gets, the more opportunity we have to keep an eye on things while offering the security and protection the people count on us for." He winks. "YOU are golden. WE are golden."
More cheers.

"Thank you," Will says, "thank you. Now I'd like to introduce two new platforms we're rolling out today that speak directly to these issues."

EWE's Army, outfitted in sharply pressed camouflage uniforms, enter the aisles, wheeling carts filled with flat boxes. They hand a box to each participant.

"This..." Will holds up a pair of glasses and puts them on. "...is Virtual Vision. You're the first to touch them outside of the development team. In a few moments, I'll ask you to put them on, but first, let me tell you about them.

"Project Virtual Vision has been in development for quite some time. They will replace every other device you now carry."

He displays a computer the size of a cigarette pack as another screen drops to the stage behind him. He turns the glasses on, and as he does, the audience sees themselves on the screen through Will's eyes. It's like being in his head.

Will turns toward The Grove screen. "SakuDoka,[44] please step forward. Delegates," he says over his shoulder, "keep your eyes on both screens. Use your peripheral vision."

At The Grove, SakuDoka stands up and moves toward the camera. As Will looks at him through the

---

[44] Minister of Arts and Entertainment, Dept. of Spin & Misdirection

glasses, on the other screen, a facial recognition program identifies him and apprises Will of where and when he met SakuDoka, how long he's known him, and how many social media connections they share.

"You can turn this function on or off," Will says as a note identified as being from Cretin appears in the upper left-hand corner: HAVE SAKUDOKA DEMONSTRATE MAN IN THE MOVIE.

"In just this brief example, you can see the value of this technology. Cretin's message instantaneously appears before me without even interrupting what I'm doing. These glasses also give you directions and timetables; can identify buildings, plants, animals, and songs; and so much more. Right on the spot, without interfering in your day."

Music swells in the auditorium and, identifying the song, the screen reads, "THAT'S THE WAY I LIKE IT" BY KC AND THE SUNSHINE BAND.

"Yes, that's the way I like it!!" Will incites the crowd.

The room breaks into a standing ovation for Will, the technology, and the future.

"Thank you, thank you... Please sit down and direct your attention to the screen for Man in the Movie."

As the lights come down in the room, *The Wizard of Oz* appears, starting mid-film, when Dorothy has already left Kansas and landed among the munchkins. As she skips her way down the yellow brick road, she comes up to Scarecrow, who tries to get her attention. But he's thwarted by Farmer SakuDoka, who has jumped into the movie.

"This is only the beginning," Will says as SakuDoka appears on both screens—at The Grove and in Oz. "We can plant stories and memory movies directly into your brain. Depression will be a thing of the past, without medication! The technology is being beta tested as we speak. So many advancements for such a great future."

The audience applauds again.

"Okay, everyone! Put on your Virtual Vision Viewers."

Will Gateways is drenched in admiration as he dazzles the audience with the latest technological advances that no one—outside of a laboratory—has been privy to before now.

"How about our musicians?" Will himself claps and whips up the audience.

Holograms of Louie Armstrong, Ella Fitzgerald, and Louis Jordan appear onstage together in full splendor, playing "What a Wonderful World."

Everyone sways and sings along as the latest tech-nological transportation advancement appears on the stage seemingly out of nowhere.

"Please welcome," Will announces, "the Holo-Deck! An achievement unparalleled in the modern world."

Inside the large black metal self-contained room, a door slides open and a group gasp fills the air. Cretin waves from inside, holographically before them while at the same time projected on the video screens standing at The Grove among the old-growth redwood trees.

"Soon we'll have the ability to transport human beings between locations in this manner. No more automobiles, airplanes, or ships! For the privileged."

"Impressed yet?" Cretin's voice rings from the stage and the forest at the same time.

Cheers abound.

"You've got TASTE!" Cretin pumps his fist in the air as he vanishes from both places.

"What's next?" Will asks Zephyr, who's waiting in the wings for the prompt. He cues EWE's Army and immediately, another group of soldiers in impeccably pressed threads enter the arena from all sides, each carrying a tray.

"Are you ready?" Zephyr asks over the loudspeaker. "Rev up your taste buds, because here comes the latest in nutritional technology. Please don't try it until everyone has their portion. I wasn't kidding about the only real food being served at breakfast."

A tempered gasp rises from the crowd as paper plates containing an indeterminable substance are passed out to all the attendees.

Will holds up an unformed block before the crowd. "The beauty of this food is that it can be made to taste like any flavor and molded into any shape or form! Chicken, fish, steak, fruit, or vegetables, pies, cakes, cookies...and there are all kinds of additives— I mean natural flavorings, to get the resemblance just right. This advancement in nutrition will soon be the primary staple food, available worldwide! Not only does it feed the people, it's cheap, easy to make, and with a stable shelf life, easy to distribute!

"Okay, everyone. Use your fingers and dig in!"

The whole room obliges. The resulting facial expressions range from "Not bad" to "No way."

"What flavor is this?" someone yells.

"What's it called?" another voice in the crowd asks.

"For now, we're calling it EAT! That's short for 'Edible Alternative Technology,' and you're sampling the unflavored version. It's mushroom spores and pea protein." Will raises both arms as the music swells to a crescendo. "You've got TASTE!" he bellows.

"Not anymore," someone screams from the crowd. Two soldiers appear in seconds, lift him up from either side, and take him away.

Upbeat music plays and streamers fall from the ceiling as Will snaps his fingers. The army returns with more food on trays, only this time, there are five little samples per plate, each formed to resemble a fish, chicken, pig, or cow, along with one designed to look like broccoli.

"And soon we'll offer earthlings the option of having their medicines mixed in. We'll call that 'M-EAT.' Clever, huh? No one will ever have to remember to take their pills again! It'll keep everyone full, nourished, and ready to go. Prescribed nutrition! Terrific, it's just terrific!"

The crowd seems almost stunned into silence.

"I know what you're thinking!" Will continues. "What are WE going to eat? What about fresh food?"

Just as he asks the question, the screen behind him displays photographs of beautiful gardens dripping with vegetables and fruit trees. The camera pans over cows, pigs, and sheep grazing freely, with chickens running around without restraint.

A dreamy voice streams over the speakers: "All employees of E.G.O. will receive benefit packages that include monthly stipends of fresh food. You're welcome to do whatever you wish with your rations. You can eat them, trade them, or sell them."

The room breaks out in a sea of sound as delegates discuss this latest development among themselves, and comments waft through the air:

"That tasted just like chicken!"

"Ahh, it's not so bad."

"I wonder what the nutritional value of this stuff is?"

"Huh?"

"Is it gluten free?"

"What's going on here?"

"I'm not so sure about this..."

"Prescribed nutrition?"

"We're serving it for lunch today," Will announces. "You'll get a much better feeling for the possibilities."

The room quiets as the convention's anthem, "You've Got Taste," fills the room. Stage lights come up slowly in dazzling colors as Angel is lowered down from a wire. She's stunning, dressed in a fitted yet flowing white dress and looking as heavenly as is earthly possible. Hypnotic music crescendos as she lands and walks to the front of the stage.

At first, Angel simply stands there, taking in the crowd as they take in her.

"Welcome, welcome! What a fine group!" She bends down and gently slaps hands with people in the front row, then stands back up and throws handfuls of wrapped assorted candy-flavored EAT into the crowd.

"We're so excited for this year's conference," Angel exclaims. "YOU'VE GOT TASTE!"

The crowd goes ballistic.

"By the end of this weekend, you'll have a whole new understanding of what's coming, and your roles in it. As a part of EWE's Army, you can be assured that even the most menial job is important... You're all vital pieces in the unfolding of the future. We couldn't do it without you. WE LOVE YOU!"

The crowd woots and applauds.

"I want to make one thing perfectly clear." She gets serious as the room quiets. "Systems appear to be crashing all over the world as we tighten the belt everywhere in the name of security. This is all by design... It's only out of chaos that a new order comes. And you're going to love it!"

The crowd cheers.

"As long as you're with us, you're family. And we take family very seriously."

Through the miracle of holographic technology, Cretin joins her onstage. Whistles, catcalls, and applause fill the hall as they hold hands and kiss.

"HAVE FUN!" Angel yells as she and Cretin wave. "You are aligned with a higher order and will be rewarded both in this life, and the next! Remember, God loves you, and SO DO WE!"

Cretin's hologram fades away while Angel does a deep knee bend.

"Before we break into groups, it's time to pump you up." Angel swings her arm around and upbeat music fills the room. "Stand up and get ready!" The crowd rises to their feet.

Angel drops her dress and Zephyr joins her, both now dressed in exercise garb. They jog in place as spotlights shine on them.

Zephyr speaks. "Announcing part of our newly implemented Health Care System: 'Group-Fit'!"

Angel demonstrates the soon-to-be-mandatory daily group exercises. For now, the program is being promoted as a way to strengthen ties and comradeship among the workers.

"It's a combination of tai chi, yoga, aerobics, weight training, and stretching. There's something for everyone!" Zephyr crows.

"We love each and every one of you," Angel preaches. "Be sure to pick up your Group-Fit progress bracelet on your way out. Soon, for convenience, you'll be able to have your progress tracking device embedded in your arm or ankle! More on that later."

"Mastery is the result of practice," Zephyr tells the cheering crowd. "Group-Fit makes the whole population *masters,* fit as an army..."

"...body, mind, and soul," Zephyr sniggers under his breath.

It's quite a sight. Board members follow Angel's lead, standing with legs spread shoulder width apart, knees slightly bent, slowly raising their arms out and up to the sky, and then bringing the energy they just raised down into their personal space. They repeat the action three times.

"This is most auspicious," says SakuDoka to the camera. "Group exercise can do nothing but strengthen us."

twenty-five

Lord takes a shortcut through the lilac and freesia garden,
savoring the luxurious fragrances. As he lifts his nose, taking
in the glory, he replays SpirIT's words in his head: *Right
attitude...eternal advancement...sees it coming.*

He's ready for advancement and appreciates the
recognition from IT, particularly during these mutable times.
Advancement from the position of Lord is epic—a glorious
year basking in the VIP section of the Galactic Order of
Relaxation, visiting coveted places, including the Infinite
Lake Resort. They have bass fishing, which he *loves.* That's
followed by one year of training in preparation for a leader-
ship role in the next cosmos. No one ever knows where
they'll be assigned to next until they arrive. It's part of the
fun, and part of the mystery.

Settling in his favorite spot, a red-velvet-cushioned
stump next to a patch of Sterling rosebushes, Lord observes
Earth via the Sheet of the World. Photographs scroll by: the
Grand Canyon; Macchu Picchu; the Zhangye Danxia land-
form in Gansu, China; Salar de Uyuni in Bolivia, one of the
world's largest mirrors; and other awesome places too num-
erous to mention. Inspired, Lord momentarily changes
himself into a hummingbird and magically inserts himself
into each landscape as it passes. He re-forms himself and
indranets Gabriel to join him.

Gabe smells a rose, then sits down on a less ornate
stump next to Lord.

"Did you catch any of Lakshmi's reading at The
Grove?" Lord asks when he arrives.

"No, I didn't, but you captured it, right? I'll study it later. I was just reviewing the ancient bet, E.G.O.'s trajectory, and how souls ended up incarnating on Earth in the first place."

"I do not know if Lakshmi stacked those cards," Lord muses, "and the only Major Arcana card, The Devil, is operating in how they see themselves. E.G.O. has cast themselves in the role of The Field on Earth—puppet masters over the population. They have replaced the Voice of The Field with the Voice of Control. Even the cards see it! Bring up the Cremation of Care Ceremony on the Map."

The hooded ferryman poling the boat across the lake toward the Owl of Bohemia comes up on the screen. Mist envelops the area. It's beautiful and eerie all at once.

"See the delusional grandeur? See the malevolence?"

"Lakshmi wouldn't stack the cards. Would she?" Gabe's eyes narrow in disbelief.

"She would not need to. Her deck is from SpirIT, and it gives accurate guidance. The narrative was just so on point. But I am afraid Cretin is not one to follow higher direction. He uses the cards for insight into us, not actions for himself and his organization."

"Life on Earth is supposed to be a vacation from the collective, albeit a working one. You could call it a treasure hunt."

Lord flashes an impish smile. "Incarnated souls are, by nature, curious sleuths. The 'work' entails asking the right questions, translating the clues, and acting on the guidance of The Field. In its simplest terms, it's 'paying attention, accepting, and allowing Providence, thus demonstrating awareness.' With Cretin doing everything in his power to replace the Voice of The Field with the Voice of E.G.O., until now, earthlings haven't had a chance.

"And it is a vacation because... Well, to put it into earthly terms, living in the eternal collective is akin being one thread in a large, woven tapestry. Yes, you can stand out, but when the tapestry moves, so do you. Incarnating in a body is indeed a vacation from that madness, like your soul's own hotel room. Even so, while your soul is ideally luxuriating in its own private space, it still thrives on connecting with others—hearing about how their vacation is going, offering opinions, etc., etc."

"Interesting," Gabe says. "So souls return to Earth again and again until they get it?"

"Yes. The more curious, receptive, and allowing one is, the quicker they advance."

"How long did it take me?"

"Lifetimes," he teases. "More than you want to know, but you did it...and that is all that matters."

"How many? What took me so long? How long did it take you?"

"Run along, Gabe. I have work to do." He winks and Gabe complies.

Tapping back into The Grove via the Map, Lord focuses in on Cretin, who's at his personal encampment receiving his daily dose of lotion. It's quite the visual—four young buff men, dressed only in fig leaf sheaths, instilling moisture into a dried-up man.

His left ear tickles. Mother Nature calling!

"Lordy, Lordy, Lord. What are we going to do with all these people trying to kill me?" she rumbles. A 2.5 quake rattles Long Beach. "Don't they know who I am?"

"You are stronger than they are, *Madre!*"

"Ahh, I'll turn 'em into compost." They giggle. "You've just had quite a run yourself, my friend," she teases. "Earthquakes, volcanoes, rain...and all at once! Mind your temper, now. I like a little sunshine touching me somewhere on my body at all times! Balance, Lord... Balance."

"Sorry for the drama. You are right, Mother. There are things I have been blind to. Huge things. But now I have full vision. Do not worry, love. It is all about to change. A plan is in place and Chip is back in your domain."

"I've been hearing you have a plan," Mother Earth replies. "I'm ecstatic the rumors are true. I've enjoyed feeling Chip's presence again. What a sweet, tempered soul."

"And we are hiring a publicist who will also serve as our Earth ambassador. Her name is Nanette Kenyon." Lord tunes the Map in to Nanette.

"She's a great choice for the G.O.D.'s ambassador. We've all been waiting for her to step up into her role."

"Her whole life has been training for this. But she still has to completely embrace and embody her gifts, tools, and wisdom. Chip is working with her. As always, I know he welcomes your assistance at any time."

"Yes, she's often quite good at listening. When *Madre Ayahuasca* [45] informed her it was time to meet, Nanette answered the call immediately. She was in ceremony with the plant within days. It was almost unprecedented, *and* Nanette still has some spots that need honing, for certain. We're on board—the land holds her, the birds are enamored with her, the plants receive her. Consider yourself supported by me and all my systems."

"Thank you, Mother," Lord says. "I appreciate your vote of confidence and, as always, your assistance."

---

[45] *Ayahuasca,* aka *La Madre* or *Abuelita,* is an Amazonian sacred jungle plant medicine ingested to induce altered states of consciousness, used with an experienced shaman or *ayahuascero* in a ceremonial setting. It is made from combining *banisteriopsis caapi* and *chacruna* or *chagropanga.* Wikipedia.

"You know we're in this together. Later, sweetheart! I bask in your LOVE."

"Adios, *Mamacita!*" Lord spins around. When he stops, he's dressed like Carmen Miranda. Taking it to the hilt, he belts out, "Mama Yo Quiero."

It's a private joke. Together, they laugh. Earth humor. Those two have always had a playful and affectionate relationship.

He changes back to his previous form while visualizing a rehabilitated planet. Being Lord, he knows how to visualize, but even as one of the most powerful beings in the Galactic Order, there are a lot of factors to pulling this off: earthlings have free will, and they must be open to being open, to receiving The Field; Nanette has to be brought up to speed; Team AWE must awaken at a livelier pace; and the deepest-set belief systems woven into the fabric of the masses must be loosened and transformed. *Yes, this is going to be a challenging, exciting, and amazing—yet difficult—feat.*

Gabe and the angels join Lord in the garden for his afternoon tea.

"Lapsang souchong?" Michael asks as he takes a sip. "Mmm, that wonderful smoky aroma…"

Lord nods. "Oh, we need more mango toast." He indranets Calissa.

Prompt as always, she arrives carrying a big tray of food. "I also brought you some banana Belgian waffles dipped in maple syrup caramel. Chef just created them from scratch." Calissa giggles. Being around Lord gives her butterfly tummy.

Lord can't help himself. " 'If you wish to make an apple pie from scratch, you must first invent the universe,' "[46] he

---

[46] Carl Sagan, *Cosmos*, 1980. Page 218

bellows. "Same applies to Belgian waffles, I imagine."
Calissa blushes. "I am teasing you, sweetheart. Thank you for
being so thoughtful."

Acknowledgement from Lord? Calissa shudders in delight as he sneezes, blowing her halfway across the room.
Somewhere on Earth, a snowstorm takes over a summer's
day.

"Wheee! That was fun!" Calissa's giddy and recovers
quickly. "It's good to be small."

"Waffles, I love waffles!" Gabe picks up a piece and
bites into it.

"How is i—"

"Shh." He holds up his hand to block Calissa's query as
she flits back and forth in front of his face. He desires silence
so he can fully immerse himself in the waffle taste experience.

Lord ignores Gabriel's request for no noise. "We just
need to reach a tipping point."

"Off the charts! Best waffle ever." Gabe reaches for
another piece.

His boss sneezes again. A hailstorm accompanies the
snow. "Must be allergies!" Lord says, although no one's
listening. They've been distracted by Calissa's new cashmere
sweater and rainbow-colored pixie cut and aren't paying
attention.

Definite faux pas in the land of Lord.

"Listen up!" He claps his hands. The angels all look at
Paschar—she keeps trying to find out where Calissa got the
sweater and if it comes in larger sizes.

Lord clears his throat, finally catching Paschar's
attention. She raises her shoulders, blushes, and bows her
head as she quiets.

Calissa flitters off. "Sorry, Lord," is heard from
underneath her breath.

Paschar knows that listening is a skill that must be fully integrated to work in close proximity with Lord. Listening tied to discovery—not in obedience, defense, or for comparison.

"As men and women on Earth begin to fully embrace the current state of affairs, some of them will gradually overstand the enormity of how off course the planet has turned. Once they grok it, those who feel called will do whatever possible to turn it around," Lord tells them.

"How *do* they shift the landscape?" Colopatiron inquires. "And how are the angels to be of service?"

"For earthlings, accomplishing change has to happen in a threefold manner. Once they learn to acknowledge The Field, they will begin to listen to Field Prompts, and then will demonstrate awareness in accordance with Universal law. They must utilize both their minds and their hearts. It is a disservice to disregard either." Lord points to the Map, now showing an animated picture of a brain and heart hugging each other. They pulse rhythmically together.

"Cretin and the Elite Global Order's campaigns have fully confused people as to what LOVE is. The mind, the masculine, has been appointed commander on high and cultivated from the earliest ages as the arbiter of truth, insight, and action. But the heart piece, the feminine, has been negated in a detrimental way."

"Whew! We're going to be busy," Michael says.

"Your job," Lord continues, "will be to assist SpirIT and The Field in tuning souls. It is a job of epic proportions. Gets challenging at times, but it is for sure to become the most coveted assignment in the Galactic Order. You are going to love it because there is no better job on Earth. Gabe, where are we in the race for souls?"

"I've calculated the numbers. Seems E.G.O.'s numbers have dropped, but they're still far in the lead. The I-don't-know-what-to-believe crowd is growing, though, which is good for us."

"Yes it is, Gabriel. Yes it is. Please give me the numbers."

"Well, Lord, there are seven point five billion people—"

"That many?"

Michael jumps in. "It seems earthlings very much enjoy the process of procreation."

"Understandably," Lord says. "We had to make it fun. Just like we had to make babies cute. You understand. I mean, really. Who would go through with it otherwise?"

The angels unanimously agree.

"Numbers?"

Gabe brings up a chart on the Map and takes out his beloved red laser pen. You can see the glee in his face whenever he gets to use it. "Four billion or so are firmly in E.G.O.'s entrapment."

Pictures flash across the Map: Corporate offices with harsh florescent lights and zombie-like workers. A crowded freeway. Live action shots of a war. Beer ads. Airport security lines. Prescription drug ads. A tax return. And a list of taxes streams down the sidebar.

The laser bounces around the screen, highlighting Gabe's words. "EGOtising has 'em right where they want 'em in every area. They worship money and material goods and have fallen hook, line, and sinker for what they have been taught life is supposed to be, never questioning it, and not going deep enough if they do."

"We will give them something to think about!" Lord waves a scepter. One never knows what he's going to do. He throws the scepter into the air, and it turns into several doves, which proceed to vanish into dollar sign-shaped money-colored glitter.

"Among the two billion or so who consider themselves 'spiritual,' not 'religious,' less than half of them understand and utilize the laws of G.O.D. And many of the rest unwittingly buy the sanitized, E.G.O.-based version of spirituality and 'jargon' their way through life. Most are easy to spot, since they 'toe the company line,' whatever the company.

"You mean the ones who talk the talk without walking the walk?" asks Nathaniel. "No fire behind them words, eh?"

"Most of them don't even know the walk," Gabe says.

"They do not Know G.O.D.," Lord says. "They know a version invented and sold to them. People are confused by E.G.O.'s Earth rules being called laws. Earthlings have been taught they need an authority…in so many areas. I find their present-day condition dismal."

"E.G.O. works both sides of the fence, pitting the New Agers against the religious, blacks against whites, rich against poor, and on and on, all the while keeping the poor mortals within a thin bandwidth of Knowing," Gabe continues. "People are stuck in dualistic thinking, fighting among themselves about this and that… Meaningless things in the big picture. Their focus is in the wrong place—"

"They are caught in a deep slumber," Lord interrupts. "It will take vigilance on our part to awaken them. Trust me, people's beliefs matter, but not for the reasons EGOtised."

The angels hang on his words. They move their chairs closer.

"Tell us," Gabe urges.

"It is important you all understand the finer tuning of beliefs," Lord says. "Take Nanette, for instance. She believes she doesn't matter, so she weighs every relationship, everything that happens to her, and every waking moment to see if she can prove or disprove this belief. Someone doesn't show up, she doesn't get the job she wants, a phone call doesn't get returned—it all gets filtered through 'I do not matter' and proves her hypothesis."

"Okay."

"So her belief that she doesn't matter shapes *her* world, not *the* world. Get it?"

"Yes. And when that belief changes, so will the world she sees, the relationships she has, the life she leads... Right?"

"Exactly."

"Fantastic!" Gabe walks over and pours himself some tea. "Earth's an amazing place! I'm going to make the sunsets all over the world extra special tonight." He pushes a couple of buttons on his watch and returns to the group.

Lord flashes her picture on the wall. "About Nanette... She is relentless in her desire to awaken, to Know the true meaning of life on Earth. Because of her undying determination to acquire the wisdom of the ages and her deep-seated Knowing that there is more to life than she and every earthling has been taught in the mainstream, she has tried everything to find the keys to unlock the doors of perception. When she is InFlow, she takes the cues, follows the signs, and does the work. When she is triggered, or has her early programming running her, she can be one hell of a bitch."

"Unbeknownst to her, she's been your student since birth," Gabe says. "When I review her history... I must say, you put her through the wringer. You must have chosen her quite early."

"Yes. All Awakened Weavers must be resilient survivors. SpirIT only invites seasoned souls to be on Team AWE. And especially to lead it.

"By the way, Nanette has finally released her I-do-not-matter belief system. She followed The Field Prompts, did the work, and cleared the issue. The path was long and lined with many clues, plants, and people guiding the way. Every living thing offers direction. Every living thing... If someone lets it."

"So true...so true," says Gabe. He knows, since he programs many of the messages.

"Chip is on his way to Nanette's." Lord nudges Gabe. "This is going to be good! She called him sooner than he thought. I am sure he thinks she is hooked, like a mighty salmon!" He roars with laughter. "We all know Chip is fond of fishing metaphors, and he is ready to reel her in. But alas, she is more like a Roosterfish.[47] It will take just the right lure to catch her."

Lord stops talking clearly trying to remember something. "Oh, wait, that was Jesus with the fishing. Seems it was the best way to communicate with the locals..."

Already on a roll, Lord produces a fishing rod out of thin air and casts it into the distance. "She has been through too much already to jump blindly into anything. She still believes she has a choice here." He laughs again. "We groomed her to have spunk. But think about it, really. Who could say no to this offer?" Lord reels in a platter of smoked salmon.

---

[47] Roosterfish: A ribbon-dorsaled fish that lives in warm climates. Powerful and very particular eaters, they prefer live bait to lures and need strong tackle to reel them in. "The 10 Toughest Fish To Catch On Artificials," James Hall, Outdoor Life.

twenty-six

The group enjoys the fish. Lord continues briefing them while concurrently grokking the information himself. There are many angles to cover with all the newfound knowledge— now that SpirIT has opened the Akashic floodgates and he's receiving cosmic downloads.

"The general population is entrained to E.G.O.'s will," Lord teaches. "If we are to be successful, we must keep ourselves in a proactive—not reactive—position.

"Preparation is the key to success, especially when someone has declared war on you. You know what war is, correct, Gabe?"

"Well, I think I'm aware of the concept…" Bewilderment washes across his face at the seemingly obvious question.

"**We Are R**ight! War is nothing but a bunch of spoiled children disguised as adults running around screaming, '*WE ARE RIGHT!*'"

The angels all high-five each other.

"I'm right!"

"No, I'm right!"

"It's WAR!" They crack each other up.

Gabe wraps his arms around them and quips, "Two shows on Saturday. Don't forget to tip the waitresses! Hilarious!"

"Yes, it is, but it is not a joke! Lucifer, Cretin, and their minions say, 'We declare WAR! We Are Right! You will listen to us!'"

Lord rages as he shakes his fist and grimaces.

"They have declared WAR on everything and everybody. The thing is, they are not right! They could not be farther from it."

"Oh, right," Gabe says. "Lay an incorrect foundation, and everything that stems from it will be skewed."

"On the other hand," Lord says, "life—to really live, to be alive—is to be a part of an openly communicative, always-changing circuit... As people AWE-waken, E.G.O. will have less and less support. The Elite Global Order will be taken down by LOVE. It was in Lakshmi's reading: the wounds that drive them will be healed."

"Aren't we saying 'We Are Right' just as much as they are? That makes us at WAR, too."

"We are not declaring war on E.G.O. War is evil. Killing for sport or gain is backward. It is no mistake that the word 'evil' is 'live' reversed. We will engage LOVE."

Lord winks at Gabe, and then matter-of-factly delivers his strategy on winning souls.

"We are simply offering present-day operating information to earthlings. Helping them expand their personal skills toolboxes, and thus furthering their standings in the Galactic Order. We give souls the opportunity for expansion. And no, we are not suggesting *We Are Right*. We are saying, 'Play with these principles and see what happens.' Our offer gains us nothing individually when laws are demonstrated, except as a collective whole."

Gabriel walks up and kisses him on the cheek. "When was the last time LOVE won over guns and insanity?"

Now the Map of the World shows scenes of indigenous tribes coming together to peacefully protest an oil pipeline. Police and military soldiers outfitted in full combat gear hose down the "protectors" with ice water on a below-freezing cold day.

"This is happening on Earth. E.G.O. is exerting its authority." Gabe shakes his head. "I'm not trying to be funny with the question, Lord. Remember the words of your favorite master of suspense, Alfred Hitchcock? 'Love, understanding, and good order are a poor defense against madness.'[48] How are we going to abate E.G.O.'s well-ingrained message?"

"To begin with, by shining light on the status quo," Lord says. "We are the Galactic Order of Demonstration! We will show them how extraordinary life is meant to be. We will demonstrate LOVE, overstanding, and unveil the meaning of being in the Galactic Order of Demonstration!

"The meaning of Hitchcock's statement is important— madness has its own resonance. You must lift it to a higher level, not defending love and goodness. Remember, Gabe, there is nothing else. LOVE is a lens—a way to see—a listening. LOVE is a field within The Field. E.G.O.'s teachings have clouded the most important features of LOVE and diluted the truth about it."

"That makes our job particularly difficult," Gabe says. "We have to introduce new meanings to words people have long used. These 'big concept words' already have contro-versy attached to them. People think they already know what LOVE is, what G.O.D. means—"

"Now, I was just about to clarify our mission," Lord declares. "You see, while E.G.O. wages WAR, we activate LOVE, the complete teaching, which has been missing from the people for thousands of years. LOVE is nothing without listening, compassion, paying attention...

---

[48] *The Men Who Made The Movies: Alfred Hitchcock* (TV movie, 1973), directed by Richard Schickel, narrated by Cliff Robertson.

"People will realize the elasticity of the LOVE FIELD. And how the truth of it has been miscommunicated, misused, and simply put, violated, really."

"How so?" Paschar asks.

"All I will say for now is LOVE has a definition. It is not nebulous, and its genuine meaning cannot be confused with any other thing. LOVE is definable; LOVE is Knowable. The Galactic Order of Demonstration is Knowable as well."

Lord contemplates for a moment.

"Souls need guidance to evolve. They need order. They need structure and direction, ritual and ceremony... So Earth is an interactive, creative environment designed to be a journey of self-discovery, fueled simply by following clues. Every living thing participates as a part of Earth's built-in interactive clues system. Plants, animals, birds, earthlings, smells, sounds... Everything!"

"Tell us more," Michael says.

"Oh, clues are revealed all the time," Lord replies, "in the form of Field Prompts. SpirIT, often with the help of IT's chief programmer, Gabriel, has many ways to communicate, including through man-made things like billboards, song titles, and newspaper headlines. And do not forget nature!"

A parrot flies into the room and squawks, "Every living thing reveals whispers, *brawk. Nam Myoho Renge Kyo.*"[49]

"I've never heard it explained quite this way," Michael says.

"A Buddhist bird?" Paschar laughs. The bird mimics her laugh and flies off. They all enjoy the moment.

---

[49] The central mantra chanted within all forms of Nichiren Buddhism. In English, *Devotion to the Mystic Law of the Lotus Sutra* or *Glory to the Sutra of the Lotus of the Supreme Law.*

"The Field," Lord continues, "is responsive, interactive, Knowable… A relationship with it brings freedom. All souls have to do is get curious about it, then listen and respond. And it is self-guided by design—the questions one asks decides the response received."

"I was just trying to remember that Buddhist chant," Gabe says, "and look what showed up! Remember, ASK/ GET! Thanks, Field, for providing the answer."

"Listening to the **W**hispers that **A**lign **V**irtually **E**verything," Lord says. "Receiving and transmitting, acknowledging—as Gabe just demonstrated—shifts earthlings into human beings, the instruments they're designed to be. Once aligned, they are InFlow."

"But…" Colopatiron starts.

"Keep listening," Lord says. "Remember, any new teaching, any new belief system, any transition on the scale of understanding to overstanding requires building the muscles to hold it, incubate it, and grow."

"Okay," Nathaniel says. "What's the difference between overstanding and understanding?"

"Well," Lord says, "it is the difference between seeing the big picture or just a segment. It is the Knowing piece in ASK/GET."

"That's right," Colopatiron says. "A snapshot never tells the whole story."

"Okay," Nathaniel says, "I understand. I mean, I overstand. I mean… I get it!"

"Do not worry, Nathaniel," Lord says. "You are receiving a lot of new information. It will all come together in one big overstanding as time passes. Understandings often come before overstandings. It is a process."

They all nod as Lord continues. "And to answer your question, Colopatiron, The Field is responsive and gives what it gets. So when Cretin and E.G.O. convince the masses to seek mediocrity, that is what they receive. Actually, it is what they want."

A group "Wow" comes forth.

"This all sounds a bit complicated," says Colopatiron.

"And Nanette? Ahh... She is perfect to present LOVE and compassion on Earth. Perfect! One learns by teaching, and she grew up in so much hate that she had to hide deep within herself. Her life up until now has consisted of pulling herself out of herself—doing her best to learn the meaning of love as it is taught on Earth and to experience the world from a different perspective than what she was raised in. It has not been an easy task; her experiences have made her both harder and softer, depending on who and what she is dealing with."

Lord waves his hand in a nonchalant fashion. As he moves, the scene he's describing projects on the wall.

"When she was little, just four or five years old, you should have seen her try to become an overstander. That little thing, trying to gain access to interdimensional Knowledge... She was so cute, and sooooo frustrated when she could not."

On the screen, young Nanette scrunches up her face and clenches her fists, trying to connect.

"'Ugh,' she cried, and vowed that she would gain Knowing. Well, when she was nineteen, a huge emotional trauma allowed entry into the knowledge she asked for. It was difficult. She had forgotten her vow and did not grok what was happening at the time. It landed her in a mental institution. They tried to keep her drugged, but she is a fighter. Anyway, all those seemingly disparate pieces, stories, and mystical bits are about to come together for her."

The little girl on the screen morphs into an adult wearing a star crown.

"Nanette is meeting herself, and Chip is helping her."

The screen changes to a video of Chip tossing Nanette a Bible and her catching it with her right, wrapped-in-an-Ace-bandage, clearly sprained hand.

"Without her long-term vigilance—her steadfast dedication to the truth, to real Knowing—it never would have happened. She opened up LOVE's lens within herself, and by doing so, she stepped into The Field. Her overstanding continues to deepen through receiving demonstrations of LOVE from others—which, remember, never needs to be qualified. Just recognized."

"Yes, we all know LOVE is unconditional by definition," Gabriel says.

"That is right! You were listening!" Lord *kvells*. "If it is not unconditional, it is not LOVE."

Just as Lord finishes his sentence, Calissa makes a dramatic entrance, delivering a tray of grilled cheese sandwiches and tea. Streamers wave off her backside and the rest of her attire is quite sparkly, along with a cashmere beret. Calissa has always considered herself a "fashionista fairy!"

Lord sneezes and a new island forms in the Pacific. "Bless you," Calissa offers. "Would you like me to get you an antihistamine? You've been so sneezy lately!" She flies closer to hand him a hanky, and he sneezes again. The new island gets a sister.

"Thank you, sweet Calissa. I am doing just fine. Now, if you will please leave us. We need to finish up here."

Calissa flutters off. Lord wipes his nose.

"How can LOVE win over guns, though?" Gabriel asks. "It's a serious question! I'm curious to hear your vision."

Lord manifests a machine gun and sprays the room with little magenta-colored paper hearts.

"Point taken, Gabe. I promise we will get back to that. On to the lesson for today," Lord says. "Go get your copies of *The Art of War*[50] and return immediately. You must overstand how Cretin and E.G.O. think and understand how they move in order to break their hold on the masses. Once earthlings get curious enough to interact and investigate higher frequencies, The Field communicates. But congruently, encrusted belief systems must be softened."

Lord throws the weapon into the air and it changes into a red-tailed hawk and flies off.

---

[50] Original Sonshi translation.

twenty-seven

Outside the convention center, people are demon-strating their unhappiness. Protesters are everywhere. Signs wave in the air, displaying the issues: **No GMOs**, **Stop Police Brutality**, **End The Corporation Nation,** and more.

Justine Maxim stands in front of a curtained-off area, rallying the troops by yelling and pointing. "Group number one, go over here. Group number two, over there! NOW!"

A person in group one holds up a sign: **When CONGRESS OBEYS ITSELF, then we can talk!**

A poster in group two reads: **Hey, LISTEN UP! First Amendment Rights.**

"TSA protesters through there," Justine shouts, pointing to a doorway in the curtain. "Keep moving!"

News cameras roll in; she hollers in their direction, "We're not gonna take it anymore!" She waves a sign: **TSA is crooked**!

Justine surreptitiously signals someone and the curtain behind her drops, revealing a fully functional, airport-style X-ray machine. Justine speeds through the full body scanner as reporters make a beeline to follow her. Actors costumed as TSA workers stop and frisk the reporters, getting very familiar with them.

Police show up in riot gear, wielding cans of tear gas and offering to send people to jail if they don't "break it up." Frisked reporters threaten to sue for sexual harassment and the scene turns to chaos.

Justine and her team are sure to record it all. Then, by refusing to leave, they get arrested. Along with several others, they're taken away in handcuffs.

***

Inside the conference arena, Angel and the crowd have completed the exercises.

"That's just a small sample of our upcoming programs." She takes a fancy bow. "We hope you enjoyed it!"

The crowd cheers, awake and ready to roll.

"Morning breakout sessions begin now," Angel announces. "Check in at the table in the back for your group assignment and exercise tracker. Volunteers will tell you where to go."

The lights come on and the crowd disperses, everyone racing toward the back, anxious to find out about their group and future.

***

Meanwhile, at The Grove...

"We'll break for thirty minutes," Cretin announces to the Elites after they complete the Group-Fit exercises along with Zephyr, Angel, and the delegates at the convention. "Meet back here lakeside for Gil's keynote address."

"Well, that certainly got my blood moving!" says Janus.

"I did enjoy that! Exercises are a great idea, Cretin," SakuDoka says. "I suggest we incorporate *chi gong*."

Cretin nods as he finds his way toward his encampment. "Changes are coming!"

Suddenly he stops walking, stands still, and looks into the distance. "Hopefully everyone will understand that they're for the greater good."

***

At the convention hall, Zephyr searches the crowd for Justine. She's always been on Cretin's radar screen as someone to watch, and now she's caught Zephyr's eye. But not for the same reason. He sees an ally.

twenty-eight

Will Gateways, finished with his presentation, leaves the stage and jumps in a private helicopter headed directly to The Grove.

Cretin awaits his arrival before beginning the afternoon's Lakeside Chat with a recap of Lakshmi's reading, which will be directly followed by the first of Gil's two talks, "Rolling Out the Future."

Once he arrives and E.G.O.'s Board of directors takes their seats among the trees, Cretin wastes no time.

"New information has been released to Lord of G.O.D. and it changes everything. As most of you know, Lakshmi's cards today were responding to the question 'How are we to proceed now that truth is in play?'"

"Ahh, yes… Truth," Gil says.

"Universal law is about to be revealed in full glory now that Lord knows earthlings never received the HOME Law Book. As you all know, not only does it reveal the Universal laws, it teaches earthlings how to genuinely navigate the Earth realm—"

"The good news," Gil interrupts, "is we still have the Power of the Lie and the Rule of the Corporation. No matter how shaken up people get, they've all been conditioned to adhere to authority. Corporate power is authority without accountability. It's fantastic."

"We used the HOME Law Book to fashion the New Testament, but maybe changed the story a little," Cretin confesses.

"Boy, once people Know the extent of their personal power... Once people know the truth..." Will muses.

"They'll never know," says Gil firmly.

Cretin smirks and raises his eyebrow. "Gil's correct. We have Time/Space Corp. and a planet full of well-trained minions. But Lord knowing everything thusly changes the game."

"Lakshmi's reading was quite revealing," offers Janus. "Remember, oracles always speak in code. The cards forebode Lord's son paying a visit to Earth again. It follows suit that we must befriend him."

"Yes," says SakuDoka. "Tangle him in our web of distractions."

"Or, as I was saying," says Janus, "hire him for a key position."

"Keep him close while keeping the masses distracted," they chant in unison.

"We're onto it," SakuDoka says. "We don't have a television *programming* department for nothing!"

"And we don't use the concept of 'programming' lightly," Janus says. "It begins at birth! SpirIT tunes, but we program!"

"We create the news, and then report on it," SakuDoka says. "I'm sure you've noticed it's all entertainment. Everything's a rivalry. The general public becomes fixated on what we tell them to!"

They pat each other on the back.

"Reality shows have put everything into the context of win or lose. The whole caboodle! Love, weight loss, cooking, 'staying on the island'... In all of it, someone wins big, someone goes home crying, and again and again, people live vicariously through the contestants

rather than going out and making stories of their own—
OR paying attention to anything we're doing. It's
perfect. We keep their attention with competitions,
serial killers, endless opinions, and celebrity nonsense."

"Well done," Cretin says. "Lakshmi related the
message to relax, regroup, and come together closely.
To keep our eyes open. Pay attention to the signs. Gil's
Lakeside Chat addresses all that."

twenty-nine

"Tomorrow we begin our sacred journey," Chip announces. "Make sure both of you are packed, because we leave for Ojai in the morning. I've arranged Otorongo's transportation; we're all set.

"Do either of you need a reminder of the proper eating required for ceremony?"

"Nope. We know the particulars quite well!" I answer. "What a great meal last night. A perfect sendoff into *dieta* mode."

"I like the way you work," Rishi says.

"That was one of the finest meals of all time," Chip says. "I'll never forget it."

"I'm so excited. I can't believe I get to sit with you!" I wiggle and squirm, barely able to contain myself. "Do you know many *icaros*?"[51]

Chip nods, the raised corners of his mouth showing his amusement. "Encyclopedic knowledge of *icaros* throughout the ages. But I am sitting *with* you. Otorongo will lead us... I humbly defer to him."

---

[51] (Quechua: *ikaro*) is a song sung or whistled in healing ceremonies used to enhance or subdue the effects of plant medicines, to evoke plant spirits, to invite the spirits of others or the deceased, to dispel dark spirits, or to protect those present, and to manage the ceremony. Wikipedia.

PART THREE

thirty

Lunch is called at CPR, and at the Center, lunch is no small deal. Think about it: How much fresher can you get than Creation? Earthly taste buds can't begin to unravel the complex nuances of nature's seasonings. Every dish is perfectly balanced in flavor, texture, and temperature.

The overseer feeds his support staff well to ensure they're nourished in every way. He knows one system affects every other system, and without a good foundation of delicious and nutritious provisions, the crew's thinking and actions might suffer. And when wrong decisions are made and wrong actions are taken in the celestial realm, there are cosmic consequences. The butterfly effect...[52]

Lord calls Gabe, Michael, Paschar, Colopatiron, and Nathaniel to the Center's meeting room.

"We have much to discuss," Lord says. "But first, let us enjoy this fare."

He doesn't believe in discussing business over food, even if that business is LOVE.

"Mealtime is for communion of food, body, and SpirIT," Lord reminds his team, "and the opportunity to receive Mother Earth and Father Sky's bounty. Lessons will begin over the beautiful dessert specially prepared for our feast."

They eat in silence, each one chewing thoroughly and savoring every bite.

---

[52] Aka the "chaos theory." Small causes can have large effects. For example, the wings of a butterfly in Japan can cause a tornado in the Americas. Wikipedia.

"We shall begin," Lord says when a cart with plates of desserts appear, one for each attendee. Each contains a bite-sized portion of tiramisu, creme brulee, chocolate lava cake, and a pineapple upside-down cupcake. They're out-of-the-galaxy delicious, with just the right amount of sweet.

"Did each of you contemplate *The Art of War* in your silence?" Lord asks.

"Yes," Paschar says, "but can we talk about LOVE instead?"

"It is as if you read my mind! We need to talk about LOVE before we talk about war!" Lord exclaims, beaming. "I love it when we are in sync!"

Just then, The O'Jays dance in from the other room, singing "Love Train." Everyone joins in. When the song ends, The O'Jays dance on out.

"I love them," says Michael.

You never know who or what is going to show up at CPR!

"Everything is clear to me," Lord says. "Now that I overstand the intricacies of what is happening on Mother Earth and LOVE's circuitous journey, we need to provide earthlings with the tools, insights, and Knowings to disentangle E.G.O.'s version of LOVE within themselves. Then they can tune themselves to the harmonies of the cosmos."

"You are so poetic," Gabe says.

"Well, words are a direct way to uncover the mystery, and a scintillating way to be understood."

"And you always pick the perfect ones!" Gabe acknowledges. "I love you, Lord."

"And I, you." Lord melts into the moment. "Ahh... LOVE."

Everyone at the table swoons.

"Disentangling LOVE on Earth is going to be one of our greatest joys and biggest challenges. It begins with our complete acceptance of the big picture on the small planet."

"This is so exciting," says Paschar.

"Tonight, I will tell you the whole story—from beginning to now—just so everyone is on the same page. It can be so easy for rumors to gain ground and mistruths to wear walking shoes with events of this magnitude. Now, we will discuss the simplicity of demonstration. Are you ready?"

"Should we take notes?" Nathaniel asks. "I'll have to run and get—"

"No. This information must be received and processed innately. I am planting seeds. No notes are required…as a matter of fact, no notes allowed. When notes are taken, a lot is missed. I want your full, undivided attention. Ready to begin?"

Hands go up around the table. Except one. Gabriel is distracted by the portable Sheet of the World on his wrist.

"Gabe?"

"Something significant is happening at E.G.O.'s TASTE Conference. Lots of lights are flickering. Will Gateways is speaking and it's activating the attendees. Folks are waking up to the truth of their existence, and not everyone is happy about it. I was just setting the Map to identify the discontents. They'll be our allies."

"Well done. Ready?"

He nods.

"First. Our beautiful Mother Earth is both heart and hearth of the Galactic Order of Demonstration. You can see it by stringing either word together…"

Calissa flies in right on cue, carrying her favorite neon blackboard. It displays the following:

eartheartheartheartheartheartheartheart
heartheartheartheartheartheartheart

She flies past Lord to the front of the room. He sneezes. Hail pelts Australia in the middle of summer from a cloudless sky. He sneezes again and in a different hemisphere, a meteor shower lights up the night.

"Bless you!" the angels say in harmony. It's always a treat to be able to authentically bless Lord.

"Notice that you cannot tell where 'heart' begins and 'Earth' ends, and vice versa," Lord continues. "And hearth, hear, ear, and art. They are all right there!" He throws sparkles into the air. "How clearly do we need to lay it out for these beings?"

Everyone enjoys the glitter as they absorb Lord's words.

Calissa flies over to Lord and he sneezes again—a new species of teacher plant appears on Earth. "I think I am allergic to you, Calissa!" he says half-teasingly. She giggles and flutters off.

Lord doesn't miss a beat. "Chip's job is to school Nanette in the seven principles of demonstration. Together they weave a tapestry of movement, growth, contentment, understanding, and purpose on Earth."

Lord pauses to sip his beverage. "The first principle is acceptance."

"It seems many of us are receiving that lesson," Gabriel says.

"Really? What do you see?"

"Well, you've got to accept that Chip didn't tell you about the Law Book and that SpirIT was in on it. Chip's going back to Earth and grooming Nanette, whose big piece of acceptance is being 'the publicist for G.O.D.' Cretin has to accept that his unobstructed rise to power is about to end."

"True, Gabriel, so true." He contemplates his team leader's words. "You have always had great vision, my dear soul." Gabe blushes.

"And what about you, my friend?" Lord continues. "Do you have anything to accept?"

"I'm a go-with-the-flow kind of guy." Gabe masterfully avoids the question. "I'll have to contemplate that one, 'cause nothing immediately comes to mind."

"Let me know when you figure something out. It is always easier to access others than yourself."

Gabe flashes an all-knowing grin.

"Can we move on, Lord?" Paschar says. "I've got to go process a group of souls who've recently arrived from Earth... Plane crash, I think."

"Okay. We just have a few more bits of information to go over. Contemplate this for the day, and tonight, after our feast, we will reconvene. Then the floor will open for questions, comments, and ideas."

Lord stands up, walks behind Gabe, and places a hand on each shoulder.

"Earthlings demonstrate their understanding of the Universal laws in every action they take, and each demonstration is a communication to The Field. Take acceptance, for example, which demonstrates clarity. When a being demonstrates acceptance, it is clear the being doing the demonstrating is no longer resisting the truth." He shakes Gabe's shoulders for emphasis. "For instance, when Nanette accepted the position as publicist, she let The Field know she was ready to receive the lessons needed to fulfill the role. As a result, The Field will provide unfettered fodder for full functionality of the principle. And acceptance activates the next step, Allowance. But acceptance is always the beginning."

"So true," says Gabriel. "I've got to accept that I've created the best Map in the history of the cosmos. That must be it."

Lord pats Gabe twice on the shoulders. "Dig a little deeper," he teases. "Maybe a lot." He returns to sit in his chair.

"Our first big challenge is for earthlings to accept that they have been duped by a gang of storytellers who only have their own unsavory interests at heart. Within that acceptance comes clarity, enabling them to learn the truth. Once they accept G.O.D. is a mechanical field—not an all-seeing, micromanaging entity—they will open themselves to working, playing, and interacting with the container they live in."

"That's a lot to take in," Michael says. "And as angels, aren't we more equipped than humans to receive?"

"Careful," the overseer says. "Angels have their own work to do, and it is not the same work as incarnated beings."

"True…" Michael says.

"Today, your assignment is to contemplate acceptance: of others, of your mission, and of LOVE as the guiding principle for human beings."

"You mean unconditional love, don't you?" Nathaniel asks.

"Again, LOVE does not need to be qualified with the word 'unconditional.' Prefacing LOVE with that qualifier is redundant. LOVE is inherently that way.

"One more thing before we adjourn. Acceptance is not only the first step in demonstration; it is the core of change and the essence of LOVE." Lord blows the room a kiss. "See you all at dinner."

thirty-one

Creaking redwoods, chirping tree frogs, and osprey calls set the stage as Cretin and his fellow Board members take their seats in the shaded grove. Gil Gamesh stands on the dais, ready to begin. A call from the Bohemian Owl brings everyone to attention and announces the meeting:

"Presenting 'Rolling Out the Future,' please welcome the CEO of the Time/Space Corporation and the leader of the purported free world, Gil Gamesh."

There's only a smattering of applause and laughter.

"Good morning, fellow Bohemians."

Gil holds up the Chinese symbol for crises and opportunity.

"I'm certain you've heard the old Chinese curse that states, 'May you live in interesting times.' Indeed, we are. But as well-known as this quotation is, it cannot be found in any ancient Chinese text and has never been traced back to China. In fact, the sentiment was written and began circulating in the twentieth century. It is thought it was intentionally constructed to sound like Confucius. Why is this point being mentioned? It's simple.

"Someone once said, 'A lie can travel halfway around the world while the truth is putting on its shoes.' Truer words may have never been spoken. Once a lie is accepted as truth, the real thing has a long row to hoe to be accepted. First truths—whether true or not—often win and hold on for dear life in earthlings.

"Lord, on the other hand, learns new truths and adjusts immediately. And truth has been revealed to Lord—with a capital T. Things will change quickly."

Gil inspects the crowd, satisfied to see everyone is captivated.

"Now that Lord's been fully informed, he's going to move steadily and swiftly to expand G.O.D.'s soul base. This travesty will be prevented."

Gil walks off the dais into the group of Board members.

"So today, the focus is on next steps. A picture of the future will be painted using the broad strokes necessary to demonstrate the overall plan. And the extent of what has occurred to quicken our work will be revealed."

He returns to the stage, takes a sip of water, and clears his throat.

"A general state of fear and distrust of 'the enemy' has successfully been woven into the general public, bringing us to a position where anything we want can be done in the name of security. All along the way, restrictive laws were legislated and passed, hidden in other bills. These laws were unrelated to the initial issues and are silently lying in place, ready to be rolled out when needed.

"People are openly being searched, tracked, and imprisoned, often for minor offenses. And most of society is either self-medicated or taking prescriptions for anxiety or any other number of disorders. Instead of genuinely helping them resolve their issues, they're covered up with psychotropic drugs, all the while creating an environment that cannot lead to anything but discontented people pretending they're content because they know no other way.

"Seeds have been patented, prisons privatized, racial tensions increased... and free speech all but eliminated. We're on track. And things have to speed up. The ties that bind must be tightened faster than originally anticipated.

"Time/Space Corp., under the guise of MEMEMEbook[53] and along with each search engine on the web, gathers metrics on everything everybody does. People unwittingly share endless amounts of personal information with no idea of the consequences. They won't recognize this until it is too late. Privacy will be all but a passing idea sooner rather than later."

A screen drops, showing the constant stream of sensitive information being culled from social media sites and search engines.

"Everything is in order for the coming irreversible societal changes to take hold." Gil wags his finger at the crowd. "Dissonance will not be tolerated.

"You members of the inner circle already know how the HOME Law Book was acquired and what happened after we got our hands on it. The brilliance of our team's work is this: Enough wisdom has been incorporated from the original message to completely sell the story, without revealing any of the true laws of demonstration or how the Earth plane really works."

Proud of his contribution and not short on ego, Cretin stands up, takes a bow, and flashes a satisfied smirk.

---

[53] Central website developed for earthlings to post every tiny detail of their lives, making them very easy to keep track of. www.MEMEMEbook.club.

Gil extends his arms toward his boss and claps his hands a couple of times. Then he continues.

"We hold overstandings that few on Earth have held in centuries: how to use the laws of The Field to demonstrate and invoke synchronicity, and how to use this wisdom to create any damn order we choose."

The men applaud.

"Everything is being rolled out one benign step at a time. You've all heard the story of the frog in the pot of water who doesn't realize he's being cooked..."

More applause.

"Now that so many believe the story we've spun, Lord and his team have their work cut out for them in getting the masses to align with their seemingly magical truths, treasure hunts, and the reality of LOVE.

"As forward motion is maintained," Gil says to the engaged group of Elites, "responsibility for toeing the company line and enforcing mandates lies with every-one. Anything less will not be tolerated."

"Who does he think he's talking to?" SakuDoka says to Janus. "We didn't achieve our status in this organization by default."

"Strong policies require strong words," Gil says, overhearing the comment. "As new procedures to increase our foothold roll out, everyone has to be on the same page, period. The slightest bit of dissension will not be tolerated. A united internal front must be maintained while a dualistic reality is presented.

"SpirIT, Lord, and his minions... Even with SpirIT's innate powers and abilities, they are no match for our strong arms. A solid infrastructure has been laid. The systems are simply being fine-tuned, any leaks sealed, and the screws tightened."

Gil makes certain he has everyone's attention.

"The playing field has radically changed. Moving forward, be prepared for direct discussions. This battle will not be lost."

There's a palpable shift in the timbre of the outdoor theater. The trees quiet and a shiver of fear and excitement moves through the men.

"Pay attention, Janus," Gil says, singling her out. "A divided, distracted, hypnotized population is the only way to maintain our power."

He moves one hand up and one hand down, again and again, miming the movements of an out-of-balance scale.

"Talking points for media distribution will cover both sides of pertinent matters—for and against—with E.G.O. representatives in both camps."

Gil goes on to emphasize that the illusion of competition in the marketplace is vital. No one must ever know that all roads lead to Time/Space Corp. The talking-point topics he lists include:

— The importance of God, Jesus Christ, and allegiance
— GMOs
— Increased regulations

"Because security and scrutiny is a small price to pay for safety," Gil says, laughing.

— Climate change
— The value of prescription drugs vs. the ineffectiveness of supplements and herbs, and vice versa

— The complete destruction of the importance
of any indigenous belief systems and the
vilification of paganism
— Terrorism
— Racial divides
— Putting inane celebrity behavior in the
forefront of all news

He scowls at the audience. "Earthlings' attentions
are so easily guided. And 'if it bleeds, it leads'[54] reigns,
which will promote an atmosphere of fear. A scared
population is a stoned audience that looks to authority
to know what to do next."
A murmur of agreement fills the room.
"They'll be so distracted by these issues that our
true intentions won't be noticed." Gil starts listing the
insider mission points.

— Continued manipulation of the press,
presenting two controlled views: (1) pro-
government, and (2) "controlled opposition"

"Oh, let me interrupt with one thing," Gil says.
"Project FF is, as of this moment, active. It includes
raising prices, lowering quality, and, in general, keeping
the populace on edge—so busy feeding and housing
themselves that they cannot focus on anything else."

---

[54] The first verifiable use of this phrase was in a 1989 New York Magazine article
titled "Grins, Gore, and Videotape—The Trouble with Local TV News" by
journalist Eric Pooley, who was angry about the quality of the local stories being
published and the sheer volume of grim stories. Pooley said, "The thoughtful
report is buried because sensational stories must launch the broadcast: If it bleeds,
it leads." Evaluatingconversations.weebly.com.

"'Fight or Flight,'" Cretin sums it up, "is what FF stands for. It's the nerve system of the future. Get it?"

The joke gets a laugh. Gil nods and continues the insider objectives, where E.G.O.'s true efforts will be expended:

— Indoctrinating children through education and religion
— Assuring corporations maintain their "personhood" status, giving them more rights than individuals
— Instilling more controls under the guise of security, which actually take away freedom after freedom
— Controlling the food supply
— Muzzling any and all people who reveal methods for anything that will reduce our ability to make a profit; organizations are in place to police, raid, and control any area, including science, health, and finances
— And last, but all-important, the meanings of "hero" and "villain" will be redefined

"In short, we are ready to roll." Gil finishes his talk to a standing ovation. A murmur breaks out among the Board as Cretin moves to the dais.

"Exciting times are afoot!" he shouts.

For a split second, his face morphs into a demonic-looking creature. Sometimes he simply can't help himself when he gets charged. He catches himself and returns to form.

"Programs continue in two hours. The next topic is 'The New Enemy,'" Cretin says, his voice raspier than usual. "In the meantime, go frolic! We must balance all this seriousness with play."

***

Gil stays behind and gazes at the lake as he sips an old fashioned, complete with maraschino cherries. Cretin joins him.

"Lord's putting together a team. Angel caught up with his son at the beach the other day. His name on Earth this round is 'Chip.'"

"No worries," Gil says, looking smug. "We have the power, an arsenal of weapons, and control of the money, the media, the military... We have the upper hand, and have for some time. We start them off young and approach their indoctrination from every direction."

"We sure do," Cretin replies. "Earthlings easily absorb what we want them to believe, without realizing it. Even the 'aware' ones! And they'll fight for something just to be right, whether they're accurate or not. If they only knew ... If they only knew." He takes a sip of Gil's drink. "Still, we must keep an eye on Chip's wanderings and neutralize any progress he makes."

He eats a cherry. A little juice dribbles down his chin.

"It occurs to me that the truth of earthling's human abilities will soon be more evident than ever before," Gil says. "We need our A game and our A players. Oh... And by the way, Cretin, watch the public morphing displays."

thirty-two

The team gathers after dinner. Lord sweeps into the Galaxy Room in the form of fire, illuminating the dangling planets and lighting the candle stars that decorate the space. Then he instantly transforms into a butterfly with one cobalt blue wing, the other clear and almost invisible—a perfect balance of seen and unseen. He darts around the room.

"Good evening, Lord," Nathaniel says. "Nice airfoil!"

The invisible wing lightly brushes Nathaniel's cheek in acknowledgement and he shivers in ecstasy. His frequency momentarily rises, evidenced by a shimmering light radiating off him.

Paschar, Colopatiron, and Michael marvel at the demonstration of affection as they take their seats. Gabe has the floor.

"Tonight's talk is on transformation by LOVE. Please direct your attention to the Sheet of the World screen."

Lord settles into his usual form, although tonight he's dressed in a purple wizard's robe adorned with small silver stars. His long, silky, salt-and-pepper hair is topped by a wizard's hat and he's carrying a crystal wand.

"I am feeling a bit like Merlin tonight," he muses, "so I thought I would dress the part." He waves his wand and white stars and sparkler sparkles fly everywhere. "Carry on, Gabe."

"You gotta love you, Lord," Michael says. "You just do."

"What do you mean by that?" Gabe asks. "When you express a feeling of love for Lord, what are you expressing?"

"Admiration and appreciation for the way he shows up." His eyes focus on the subject being described. "For your ability to be yourself; a walking demonstration of self-embodiment and a beacon of confident movement. It's no wonder you are Lord."

"I will get you later." The overseer winks at Michael.

"Are admiration and LOVE the same thing?" Gabe asks. "They've been co-mingled in the Earth realm..."

"On Earth, I've been received as an Angel of Miracles," Michael replies. "The truth is, however, there are no miracles —only unknown laws. Earthlings use the term 'miracle' to describe the indescribable, the things they don't understand. I would prefer to be called the Angel of LOVE, because the deployment of true LOVE is the biggest miracle of all. In answer to your question, Gabe, what I just expressed about Lord is admiration, but The Field in which it was spoken is what I consider LOVE. When I convey LOVE, it means I see you through the lens of you, and I listen to your vibration without the filter of my own conditions."

"But is it possible, Michael, to receive another without filtering them through your own experience?" Lord asks.

"If LOVE is a field, it's always there to attune to. When one being expresses LOVE to another being, it's recognition of the other being's ability to tune them. Yes. I'll go with that for now."

"Nicely put!" Paschar jumps in. "I feel LOVE for you in hearing your response. Thank you." She blows Michael a kiss.

"Can you all feel the viscosity of the LOVE Field present in the room?" Lord asks.

"Oh, yes," Colopatiron says. "More, please."

"Gabe, continue." Lord waves his wand in his direction. This time the stars, hearts, and sparkler sparkles are red, purple, silver, and gold. Sometimes Lord is so fancy.

"Your conversation leads in perfectly to my talk tonight," Gabe says. "LOVE is so much more than earthlings allow it to be. You see...

"The concept, meaning, and demonstration of love have long been co-opted by Cretin and E.G.O., twisted into a form that tarnishes the whole realm. As with so many things, once a false foundation has been laid, E.G.O.'s work is done. The prescribed concepts root themselves into culture and everything grows from there."

He directs everyone's attention to the Map, now featureing EGOtising's romanticized version of love and beauty. As he walks toward it, the image changes to a picture of a brain. He touches the screen and the brain begins firing. "They go as far as to employ neurobiologists to figure out how to bypass the conscious mind."

"May I comment on that?" Paschar asks.

Gabe nods.

"In my role on Earth as Dissolver of Illusions, I've noticed that people don't realize how their beliefs and what they accept as true—or not—shapes their lives. The teaching that acceptance is recognition, not resignation, is a good place to begin, because once something is recognized, it's available for change, reinterpretation, revolution...and for demonstration, once it's been explored."

"Bravo, Paschar." Lord applauds. "Gabe, please continue."

"The Sheet of the World shows us that as the Powers That Be tighten the belt of E.G.O.'s laws, some people are questioning the prescribed order—things they've blindly accepted for a long time. Other people seem to get more and more entrenched. But we have SpirIT and the power of the Galactic Order working for us, and with the help of Nanette, Chip, and you, and the AWE-wakening of Team AWE, truth will spread like the fire Lord appeared as here tonight. What does this have to do with LOVE, you ask? Everything."

Lord shoots a ball of fire across the room, which fizzles out before it hits anything. "What a master!" Nathaniel says.

"Well spoken. Now talk about what LOVE is, and how we will proceed."

"Happily," Gabe says. "LOVE is a field within a field. Lord says that as a noun, we're to focus on the L being a lens. But when it's a verb, the L stands for 'Listening.'

"First, what's a lens?" Gabe is taking his role as teacher quite seriously. "It's way of seeing. An object or device that focuses, or otherwise modifies, the direction of movement of light, sound, electrons, etc. The LOVE FIELD offers a viewing platform to live life through and a focus to those who actively use it. You don't need to remember this piece, but it's kinda fun. The contemplation for LOVE FIELD is Lens Opening Virtually Every Frequency/Freedom In Earth's Linear Dimension. Listening opens freedom as well. And once you embody the feeling, it will live you as much as you live it."

"Beautiful teaching." Lord clangs a gong and they bathe in its resonance. "Ready to talk about the plan?"

"Ahh, yes… This is so exciting!"

Gabe continues. "As you all know, Nanette Kenyon is the Galactic Order of Demonstration's new publicist on Earth. Chip's working with her now to bring her abilities up to speed, clear out the residues of false understanding, and align her with our mission. This isn't occurring against her will; she's indicated her readiness by setting the intention to clear out her past. As one smart cookie and a dedicated spiritual warrior, the woman listens and sees through the lens of LOVE as often as possible, but when she gets triggered, all bets are off. Luckily, she has the support of her friend, Rishi, who's been a witness to the whole invitation and initiation process. So Nanette has a sounding board who knows this is really happening and that she's not crazy. Rishi is her anchor, and she needs one!

"Chip, Rishi, and Nanette are going into ceremony together. Nanette will learn more about living in LOVE during that journey, and when they return, she'll be primed for the next phase: working together with our ambassadors on Earth to trigger Team AWE toward operating at the next level. This will have a chain reaction in gaining souls and reducing the hold Cretin and E.G.O. have."

Gabe takes a breath. "Questions?"

"What's next?" two of the angels ask in unison.

"Simply listening," Gabe says. "And contemplate the teaching of LOVE. With contemplation comes recognition, acceptance, and wisdom."

"How are we waking up Team AWE again?"

"They have triggers that are different for each of them," Gabe says. "It could be a glance from someone, something they read, a chance encounter, some little whisper or nudge, a teaching... Then, all of a sudden, they awaken and resonate on a higher tone. The process takes years, yet it happens in an instant. You'll recognize it when you see it. People have been waking up and joining Team AWE for centuries. Now it's time to rattle the masses. We'll track the AWE-wakenings on the Sheet of the World. They're beautiful to witness."

"And once Nanette learns how to listen on an even deeper level," Lord says, "she will be able to receive instruction and begin operation on an unfathomable scale, waking up AWE en masse. These are really exciting times."

"Nice," Paschar says. "And so true."

"One more thing," Lord offers. "SpirIT's intent is to provide all incarnated souls with every possible clue to grow into their next advancement. They must be curious enough to seek them out, though, and open enough to listen. Life on Earth is most definitely a collaboration with the cosmos. As of now, there are no excuses for the population of Earth to stay asleep and not wake up."

Lord hits the gong with a fringed mallet. The sound reverberates through the room, through CPR, and sends a wave through the cosmos, which is visible on the wind by those who can see. As the gong fades, Earth, Wind and Fire appear, singing the song "That's the Way of the World."

thirty-three

Gil's second Lakeside Chat, "The New Enemy," is well underway.

"Manipulation of public opinion is simply one of the by-products of the times. Departments need to be briefed. Upcoming changes to policy will result in new guidelines to be followed."

He paces back and forth across the stage, then stops midway. He whips his fist forward, his voice getting louder and louder with every sentence. "Terrorism is now defined as speaking out against our policies or our God. Empty camps are waiting to be filled. Censorship rules the day. We will not be defeated!"

Gil lowers his arm and regains his composure. "Everything is clearly laid out so there can be no confusion. Pay attention."

His eyes look up to the left, reviewing his mind and checking to see if there's anything else. There is.

"One more thing." Gil traces the Sign of the Cross on his body. "The God in the sky was created deliberately to divert earthling's attentions away from Mother Earth and her built-in messages." He holds up a small version of a flexible geodesic dome. "If you read the suggested conference pre-reading, the truth behind the structure of the matrix is now known."

He tosses the dome out into the audience, then genuflects. "When they're looking up and praying, they're missing the whispers right before them. It's all right in front of them by design. The ultimate misdirection has been pulled off."

Gil generates three coins and masterfully performs a few close-up magic tricks. "Everything's going according to plan. Earth-based cultures squelched. Indigenous tribes corralled, their ways discredited. Their teachings continue to be suppressed. The people of Earth will never know the truth about their existence. Never! We must stay united. Thank you. Questions?"

Just after Gil opens up the floor, Cretin quietly excuses himself to attend to an issue at the TASTE Conference. It seems Zephyr has gotten into it with one of the security guards.

Cretin views the incident through the holo-cam. His conviction that Zephyr's finished in the Elite Order is cemented. He will not put up with this level of dissension, and he's certain Lucifer will agree.

"Bring her to me," Zephyr demands as Cretin watches. "I want to see Justine Maxim, and I want to see her now."

"I'm sorry, sir. I have my orders, and they don't come from you," the security guard replies. "She's being held in jail for her complete disregard of protocol and for her lack of concern for the safety of convention attendees. Go bail her out if you want to see her."

Cretin's amused by the security guard's disrespect for Zephyr's position. Walking toward his camp, Cretin makes a mental note to give the man a bonus. Just then, a hawk sitting in a nearby tree drops a rat carcass from above.

"You know I'm the executive producer of this event, right?" Zephyr continues on the holo-cam.

"I'm sorry, sir. I've been given my orders and they don't include bringing that woman to you. I don't mean to be disrespectful. I can only act on orders. Just doing my job."

Cretin calls Zephyr while observing him answering the phone. "How's everything going, Busy One?" He doesn't let on he knows what's happening.

Zephyr is curt. "What can I do for you?"

"Nothing. Just thought I'd check in."

***

"I've got to go." Zephyr hangs up. He blocks his phone number so it can't be recognized and calls Justine on her cell phone. When he gets her voicemail, he doesn't leave a message.

He moves toward the horde of protesters and news teams in front of the building, all the while gathering the internal strength to step into his future. He knows this is the end of his charmed-albeit-troubled life.

Then, surprising himself by discovering he's no longer able to toe the company line, Zephyr makes a radical move. He opens the convention site doors and invites the press and protesters into the conference. With the throng clamoring through the doors, he walks off the grounds and heads to the jail to spring Justine.

***

Cretin returns lakeside just as Gil finishes answering the last question. He takes him aside.

"There's a helicopter waiting to take you the convention. It's chaos over there. The holo-cam shows Zephyr let the media in..."

"We own them, Cretin. It's okay!"

"No, it's not. You know we feed them what we want 'em to know, scripted and ready to go. Seeing behind the scenes, where they can form opinions for themselves, is unacceptable. That insubordinate brat opened the doors and simply walked away! The good news is he's cemented his future and we won't have to deal with him anymore. The bad news is, he knows so much. Lucifer will never let us 'take care of him' in an appropriate manner."

"How should we handle this?" Gil ponders. "Ahh—I know...distraction. Let Angel know the bomb threat they're about to receive isn't real."

"I knew I loved you," Cretin says.

Gil leaves for the conference. The troll-man calls Angel, then turns and addresses the group. "Change of plans." He briefs them on what's happening at the conference site.

"Is Gil going to plant a bomb?" Janus asks. "Isn't that a little extreme?"

"He'll do whatever it takes." Cretin moves his arm in an arc and snaps his fingers. "We reconvene in an hour to discuss how to move forward."

***

Janus scurries back to her camp and contacts her executive news producer, Harry Delman, who's onsite at the convention. "Bomb threat leads. Allude to terrorism. Make sure everyone's attention is on security, not the purpose of the conference. Use your best diversion tactics, Harry. Your job depends on it. My cell phone is on."

Just then, a large explosion is heard over the phone line. "I gotta go," Harry says. "A bomb just went off!"

Speechless, Janus hangs up the phone, her face white as a ghost. "He didn't..."

***

Zephyr and Justine hear the explosion from miles away and head back toward the convention center. "Cretin's responsible for this," he says. "And we've got to work together to expose the truth."

"That's all I've ever wanted to do. But you know more about the truth than I do—on many levels."

"All will be revealed. It's important you know that I've left the Elite Global Order. The good news is that I'm safe from harm. My parents won't allow anyone to hurt me without grave consequences. The bad news is that I've been cut off from all the resources previously available to me."

"Everything will be fine, Zephyr. I've had my eye on you for a long time. As long as we're working together, I've got your back."

thirty-four

Lord, Gabe, and Chip converse via the Map about the team's upcoming ceremony. Lord downloads a few important understandings about Nanette's life so Chip and Gabe can be properly supportive of her during and after the ritual.

"This is going to be the most intense ceremony she has participated in to date," Lord advises. "All the previous ones have been leading up to this one. *La Madre* has been showing our girl the incredible hold her mind has on her experiences. She is about to be given the keys to her heart. She will still need to do some clearing work to use them, though."

"I'm participating in the ceremony, no?" Chip asks. "I won't be of much help to her if I'm busy having my own experience. You know the guidelines of Shamanic ritual."

"Trust me, my son. You do have some work to do yourself!" Chip blows him a kiss.

"The information is for support on the other side, not during," Gabe says. "SpirIT has important teachings for all three of you."

"Nanette's intention to enter the second half of her life with a fresh start is the impetus for her ceremonial purge," Lord adds. "And Rishi is in the beginning stages of working with plant medicine—still meeting herself. She does not know what she does not know. This journey will give her an inkling." He looks fondly at his beloved offspring.

"You, son... Well, we will talk after. Go now and prepare for this earthly Awakening. *La Madre* brews for your ceremony right now as Otorongo prepares for your journey. If you listen to the wind, you might even hear his songs. He may appear in your dreams."

Suddenly, pastoral music fills the air and the ceiling is washed in colors akin to the northern lights. "I must go. SpirIT is calling me."

SpirIT connects with Lord and instructs him to go into his private chambers for a teaching and a "come to Jesus" conversation. SpirIT has a sense of humor, too.

"Chip's listening well and has really stepped up into his position on Earth. Good job on your part. I know the whole earthlings-never-received-the-Law-Book thing really threw you for a loop, but I'm here to tell you that you received the information well and adjusted to the new plan in a way that lets me know you're the one for this job. I always knew you would show your teeth at the appropriate moment. Good job! You clearly overstand what's happening. There's one piece I want to make very clear, though."

"What is it, Great One?"

"You must give this final push for souls your all. The future of the planet's not the only thing on the line here. Your future is as well."

"I hesitate to ask, but what are the consequences of failure?"

"Hush. Not an option." IT pauses. "Don't even consider it."

Lord stands up and smiles nervously. "Do you have time for a tuning?"

SpirIT obliges. He plays a certain combination of brass and strings.

"You're doing well. You have more plates spinning than you realize. Indeed, the Mystery gets greater and greater with every moment. I have more faith in you and your abilities than you could ever know."

"Thank you, Great SpirIT. I trust from your words that all will be revealed in time."

"So it will be, my Lord. So it will be."

thirty-five

Chip, Rishi, and I drive by car to Pepper Tree Retreat, formerly Krishnamurti's estate, which is nestled in the east end of Ojai. About an hour and fifteen minutes outside of Los Angeles, it's the perfect place to sit together in ceremony. Chip arranged for us to rent the entire retreat center for a whole week. It is good to be the son of Lord and have unlimited funding.

On the way there, we stop to get gas. I pump while Rishi heads to the bathroom and Chip goes inside the station. He comes out with a small package. Rishi joins us and we get back on the road.

"Nanette, tell me about your relationship with tobacco," Chip says, pulling a bag of organic American Spirit Tobacco out of the sack. "How would you describe it?" "He opens it and rubs the fresh, moist strands between his fingers, filling the car with a sweet, musty scent. He tosses the tobacco pieces out the window while thanking Mother Earth for this beautiful day.

"Funny you should ask. I definitely have one!" I reach into the sack, take a few strands myself, smell it, and toss it out, too. "I've found that tobacco has been misused by the general population, and then demonized for the effects of the user's excessive ways."

"Nice," Chip says.

"And I was in the same boat. I started smoking young and smoked cigarettes for ten years until I proudly quit on February 4, 1984, at 5:04 p.m. Ha—I remember! And it wasn't easy.

"I'll never forget the moment I knew I was finished smoking for good. I worked at a rock 'n roll nightclub in San Francisco called The Stone, which also owned a record label and PR company. The club booker and I both wanted to quit, so to make it fun, we bet each other a fully paid ski trip to Tahoe for two. You had to quit using anything made of tobacco for six months. If either one of us smoked, we lost the bet. It was the honor system. The Fourth of July was judgment day.

"Three weeks into my non-smoking foray, a couple of friends and I went to a work function—an album release party for Eddie Money at a sports bar in Pacifica.

"We were drinking and doing cocaine and partying up a storm. My friend Angie was my ride home. On the way out, I bummed a cigarette from someone. I moved the cigarette back and forth underneath my nose, taking in the aroma. When we got into the car for the twenty-five-minute ride home, I tried to find the lighter.

"'It doesn't work,' Angie said.

"I searched the car for matches. I searched my purse. As high as I was, in a moment of sheer undeniable magic, I suddenly stopped searching amid a moment of incredible clarity.

"'What the fuck am I doing?'

"I broke the cigarette in half, threw it out the window, and declared myself a non-smoker. And I was. That was it." I snap my fingers.

"But just like when I used to dream I ate peanut butter during fasts, or that I'd gotten up and gone to high school and then woke up in my bed during fourth period, I used to dream that I still smoked." My leg starts shaking. "Throughout time, I've felt confused. I knew I quit smoking years ago, and yet in waking hours, I felt I still smoked because I dreamt it so often. Sometimes I have trouble differentiating between sleeping dreams and waking reality.

"It was only after I answered the call from *Madre Ayahuasca* that I began to forge an honest relationship with tobacco in this dimension." My leg stops. "I was being smudged for a ceremony and the facilitator leading the circle said to me as he worked, 'Tobacco likes you.'"

"What's not to like?" Chip beams and I blush in response.

"During this phase of my life, I participated in quite a few ceremonies during a short period, including a sweat lodge, a flower ceremony, and many sittings with *La Madre*.

"Hearing the facilitator say the words, 'Tobacco likes you,' along with my recent experiences with Shamanic ways, opened me to a new relationship with the teacher plant—evidenced by what happened at the sweat. After we tied the black, red, yellow, and white prayer ties and the firekeeper stoked the fire, heating the rocks, we made our own tobacco offerings to the lodge leader and were ready to begin. Sage smoke surrounded us as we crawled into the covered structure clockwise from the east. Gobi, who led in the Miwok tradition, lit and passed the ceremonial pipe.

"You don't have to take it to your lips," he offered. "If you're not comfortable smoking, tap the stem once on each shoulder and pass it along." The pipe came to me. I wasn't sure what to do. Then I knew. I heard sacred tobacco's spirit ask me to smoke him. Even though he hadn't crossed my lips in over twenty-five years, I didn't hesitate.

"After the sweat lodge, I got myself a sack of organic tobacco and began rolling my own smokes. This went on for a month or so, but I found myself not enjoying the undertaking. My lungs didn't like the smoke and my head often felt dizzy."

"You weren't using the tobacco ceremoniously, were you?" Chip asks.

"Well, I told myself I was. But I was fooling myself… I inhaled! There was so much I didn't know. But The Field always seems to have a way of guiding me to the right action. I keep seeing this truth more and more. There is so much I *don't* know!"

Both of my friends nod in agreement.

"Just about this time, a new acquaintance who called himself Merlin gave me a ceremonial pipe. I accepted and smoked tobacco in it, but something still didn't feel right. So I put the pipe down and didn't interact with it for a few months.

"Then I went on a plant medicine retreat. As I was about to leave, I heard the pipe tell me it wanted to come. It's easy to disregard these little nudgings, but I was and am always practicing listening, and so I packed the pipe in my suitcase.

"One day during the retreat, I pulled it out, went around the fire circle, stuffed it with tobacco, and started smoking. I offered it to people around me, wanting to share my tobacco and the moment.

"I noticed one of the other participants, a man named Ira, watching me from a distance. He got my attention and asked about my pipe. I told him how I acquired it and admitted that I really had no idea what I was doing."

"He said he could tell. He also said he could feel the pipe, and told me the spirit had left it long ago. He said the pipe needed to be buried for a prescribed period. I could do it myself, or he would be willing to do it for me.

"I contemplated his offer. As I did, he stated he was being guided to make me a new personal pipe. He also mentioned that the one I had was male. I asked him how he knew and he pointed to the long end piece protruding from the bowl. 'Female pipes are L-shaped, and males are T-shaped. Spirit's telling me to make you a pipe,' he said, 'and to teach you how to use it.'

"We completed a ritual exchange for the pipe and Ira said he would send me mine when it was ready.

"Almost exactly one year later, I received a text from him: Your pipe's on its way. Call me when it arrives and I'll guide you through its initiation."

"Nanette, that's quite a story," Chip says. "Initiation is such an important piece in every new endeavor."

"And it's skipped over so often," Rishi adds. "As the world moves faster and faster and technology grows and grows, initiatory practices get left behind."

Agreement resonates among us.

"So I received the pipe and called Ira. 'Your pipe has turtle medicine,' he told me.

"He went on to describe the ceremony I was to perform with the pipe—every day for twenty-eight days.

"'You and your pipe will get to know each other,' Ira said. 'Tobacco can be as powerful a teacher as *Ayahuasca*.'

"So my relationship with my pipe began. We met every morning around the same time for twenty-eight days, and together we prayed to the seven directions. One of the things I learned from my initiation with my pipe is that praying has much more to do with listening then I ever realized."

Just then we see the retreat center driveway on our right and turn in. We collect our belongings and walk from the parking area to Pine Cottage, one of the group meeting spaces.

"We're here to empty," Chip says. "To allow ourselves the space and time to receive the messages Mother Earth and Father Sky have for each of us. In order to fully give ourselves to the experience, we've got ourselves a cook."

We look in a large picture window and a beautiful Jamaican woman waves a fish at us and smiles a big toothy grin.

"Wonderful news! I wondered how I was going to prepare our food while immersing myself in other dimensions," I reply. "Thank you. You spoil me."

"Just curious, dear one. What had you decided you were going to do?"

"I only thought about it for a moment. Then I let go and knew all would be taken care of. Everything would fall into place. I decided to acknowledge the prospect of allowing ease."

"You're learning." He bends down and picks a single buttercup and lupine. With eyes sparkling, he hands them to me.

I notice Rishi taking in the teaching at the same time a gentle breeze whistles through the trees, touching us all with the feeling of grace. "More synchronicity from SpirIT," I say.

"Let's get settled into our rooms and spend the next few hours exploring on our own," Chip suggests. "We'll meet back here at Pine Cottage for dinner. How's six?"

"Sounds good to me."

Rishi agrees. "Here's a map to the property and surrounding areas," she offers. "So much beauty!"

"Let's be sure to take in the sunsets here," Chip says. "They're rare and special. We're in one of the few places in the world to experience 'The Pink Moment' as the sun goes down. Enjoy the grounds. See you at dinner."

***

Our evening meal at Pepper Tree is simple yet delicious. No salt, sugar, spices, garlic, nothing fermented—just green bananas, fish, plain rice, steamed veggies…This clean food was clearly made with love.

"Ready for your surprise?" Chip asks. "Any guesses?"

"You're not really a representative of G.O.D.?" I tease.

"Ahh...nope. That's not it." He smiles. "You, Rishi?"

"Not a one. There are way too many things you could surprise us with."

They affectionately bump fists.

"Okay. The surprise is, Otorongo sent us master plants to work with. He was guided by SpirIT to amend our ceremonies." Chip pulls individually sized and labeled bottles of different colored viscous liquids out of his bag and places them on the table. "Starting tomorrow morning, we'll sit in silence with ourselves for the next few days until he arrives."

My face lights up. Rishi wiggles and claps.

"Tell me about your experience with master plants." Chip looks in my direction.

"I drank Ajo Sacha in Tarapoto—a brown liquid with a mild garlic taste, not unpleasant. I was told it's good for feeling rooted on Earth, that it's a blood purifier and cleans your energy." I take a swig of water from my bottle. "There were mystical experiences during the short five-day *dieta*. One day I awoke from a nap in a state of bliss. The plant told me I was enveloped in pure unadulterated life force energy. It was only for a moment, but I'll never forget that sense of peace in my body, mind, and spirit. I also learned from the *curandero*[55] that it's considered 'jungle technology.' Hunters drank it before going into *la selva* so they didn't smell human and the animals wouldn't know they were coming."

"It also helps relieve the effects of shock, Nanette. Ajo Sacha was a good first plant *dieta* for you after all you'd been through."

---

[55] Traditional native healer or medicine woman or man.

245

"I wanted to stay in the jungle for longer—much longer —but alas, it was not in the cards...or should I say 'the wallet' at that time."

"You're aware of *how* they work?"

"Plants' spirits communicate with open beings; each has their own unique qualities and healings to offer. We can learn so much from them: how to strengthen our hearts, sacred ways to communicate with our mind and spirits. They teach us their songs, how to cure our bodies, and they test us in our dreams. They often work in tandem with *Ayahuasca*."

"And how do the plants communicate?"

"Through dreams, visions, and through feeling states. Their energy becomes you—it's a fusion. They clean you. A master plant affects your way of seeing."

"You've received a lot of Knowledge on how they work. And there is more to Know."

"I've been wanting to partake in a master plant *dieta* for some time," Rishi jumps in. "This is exciting, and a wonderful surprise."

"At some point I would like to do a thirty-day *dieta*," I say.

"The unfoldment of the future is a mystery, but the possibility is always there," he responds.

"What plant are we drinking?" I ask.

"We're all drinking different medicine since we're in different places on our journeys. Otorongo sent Ajo Sacha for you, Rishi." He points to a bottle and she pulls it toward her. "Ushpawasha Sanango is for Nanette..." He hands me mine. "...and he sent a special combination to help me reorient to Earth as she is today, and open my channels to align with her communications." His bottle sits before him.

"What are the properties of Ushpawasha Sanango? Do you know why Otorongo chose her for me?"

"I've been instructed to allow the plant to teach you, Nanette. He will tell you everything you need to know about him. Yes, the plant is masculine."

"I'm going to pay attention to him. I'll listen."

He whispers to me loudly, "It's always good to listen to your teachers." He turns to leave. "Sleep well tonight, my Earth angels. And enjoy tomorrow's silent contemplation. Your meals will be delivered, so you can go deep."

***

After a day and two nights of unadulterated silence, as the morning light streams in through the cabin window, I'm pulled out of a deep, dreamy sleep by the sound of a vehicle, followed by voices. *Otorongo!*

I throw on a comfortable sarong that's just the right weight for the beautiful sunny day and head outside to greet the master shaman, his interpreter, and Chip, who I see has already welcomed them.

"¡Buenas días, Maestro! ¡Y Tatiana!" I say. "Estoy tan feliz de ver qué usted."

Otorongo, happy to see me again too, throws his arms around me. "*Ha pasado demasiado tiempo*," he says to me. "Too long."

"Tatiana! What a wonderful surprise!" I embrace the full-blooded Latina who was the interpreter on my trip to Peru several years ago, and is now my soon-to-be Spanish teacher! We became instant friends and stay in touch, but I didn't know she was coming. Now Rishi will finally get to meet her in person. This adventure just keeps getting better and better.

"Good morning, Chip!" I say, hugging him enthusiastically.

"¿Se va a reunir otra?" Otorongo asks.

"There is another lady joining us?" Tatiana translates. Just then, Rishi emerges from her cabin.

"Rishi, meet Otorongo, our heralded *maestro*," I say.

"Buenos días, mi amor," Otorongo says. "Es un placer conocerte."

"Good morning, my love. It is a pleasure to meet you." Tatiana translates flawlessly, as usual.

"*El gusto es mío,*" Rishi responds.

We both have limited abilities in Spanish, and I've not yet begun my birthday gift lessons. I throw my arms around Tatiana and Otorongo again.

"La planta medicina dieta," Otorongo says. "¿Qué tal le va?"

"The plant medicine has been good," Rishi says. "I'm just beginning to be able to hear its messages for me. Inklings…or make that seedlings!"

"*Paquarina,*" Otorongo says.

"The word '*paquarina*' means place of birth, new beginnings, or origins," Tatiana says. "It's where the sun rises."

"Beautiful!" Rishi responds.

"I've had very active dreams," I say. "Lucid and enlightening. And a strong feeling about our coming ceremonies—sitting with *La Madre* in combination with the master, Ushpawasha Sanango. I'm loving his teachings."

"Thank you for my brew, *Maestro*," Chip says. "It's opening up new channels in understanding and overstanding. Mother Earth is ready for change, and she's clear about the path."

Tatiana translates for Otorongo's ears. Then she speaks to us. "Otorongo has traveled far and would like to rest. He's happy to be here, and so am I. May we please be shown to our rooms?"

Just then, our robust cook, Jodeann, appears with a tray of young coconuts cracked open, ready to drink with straws sticking out. She hands each of us one, then gestures for Otorongo and Tatiana to follow her. We're all safe in her good hands.

thirty-six

Cretin meets the Board lakeside to give orders and receive news.

"This turn of events gives us fear leverage over the general populace. We will use it in our favor. Any updates?"

"We're amping up the terror angle," Janus informs him. "All news outlets are focusing on who could have done this to us, and SakuDoka is producing the event storyline and talking points to distribute to the networks —everyone must broadcast the same spin. Continuity!"

"Stay on top of it." Cretin glares. "This meeting is adjourned. Go back to your posts and keep the lines of communication open. Be prepared for anything."

***

After grabbing a snack, Cretin heads to the great room in the lodge and turns on the news.

While no one has claimed responsibility for this act of terror, indicators point to factions from the Middle East.

Video of some previous, unrelated war effort flashes on the screen behind a very earnest-looking reporter.

It's not known yet if there are any casualties from the explosion. We have been advised to instruct you to stay away, as the area is off limits to the unauthorized.

A hotline number has been set up for you to call about information regarding your loved ones.

The number scrolls across the bottom of the screen.

And in other news, the woman who claimed she saw Jesus on a piece of toast last week is being committed to a state hospital for further observation.

E.G.O. does what it does best—comes together to knit the lies and misdirections that maintain their stronghold on society.

thirty-seven

On the morning of the first *Ayahuasca* ceremony, Chip,
Rishi, and I convene for the first and last meal of the day—
fish, rice, plantain, and herbal tea. I get up and begin pacing.
"No matter how excited I am about sitting in ceremony, I
always have a certain level of trepidation. Anticipation is
such a beast!"

"What worries you about it?" Chip asks.

"Don't scare me!" Rishi jokingly plugs her ears and
starts chanting "Nah nah nah..."

"The smell of the liquid alone nauseates me. It's funny.
The first time I drank, I was near the end of the circle, so I
got my medicine close to last. I watched the first person—a
young, pretty woman—sit before the shaman to receive her
brew. Before she drank, her face contorted in a way that
made me think she felt something heinous was about to
happen. It was clear it had to do with the taste. Other people
had similar reactions. When my turn came, I was surprised
that the taste of the liquid didn't offend me. The viscous brew
passing through my lips tasted earthy, almost sweet. Not like
anything I'd had before. But after participating in ceremony
after ceremony, I now have the same gut reaction as the
woman from the first night. The taste became vile, once I
knew what was coming.

"So first, there's that. Second is the actual purging, the
visions, and the plant's teachings. Every ceremony is different and, as much as I want to be, I'm not so good at letting go
of control and allowing. It's something I need to improve on.
Even though I've left every ceremony better off than when I
began, the unforeseen events between the start and the finish

leave me apprehensive. When I was participating frequently, each time, I experienced less trepidation. But I haven't been in ceremony in several years, so I'm a little nervous." I glance at Rishi knowingly. "Did I scare you? Are you ready to bolt?"

"I'm outta here!" She pretends to get up to run away. "Nah—you and I've been wanting to sit together for a long time. You know me. Once I've signed up for something, I see it through. I'm ready to meet her."

"Good thing, because she's also ready to meet you!" Chip reassures her. "And we'll be well taken care of with Otorongo, Tatiana, and Jodeann feeding us and assisting with the ceremonies. It's time to begin."

Finally, the first night is here. The yurt housing us for the ceremony, our *Maloca*,[56] is the perfect size for our group—intimate, yet roomy enough so we're not on top of one another.

Jodeann has taken care of setting up the inside, making sure everything is in place. Our personal areas are draped with a four-pelt sheepskin, pillows, blankets, a bucket for purging, and a bottle of water. And we all have back jack chairs in case we want to sit up comfortably during the night.

Sunset nears. We meet at the *Maloca*, ready for the night's journey.

The First Ceremony

Otorongo stands outside the yurt, blessing and cleansing us as we enter, using tobacco as his medium. As we pass, he blows smoke from every direction, purifying and readying us to meet *Ayahuasca* herself.

"*Limpia, limpia,* clean, clean."

---

[56] Traditional ceremonial space

He enters the yurt, takes his place in the circle, and prepares the medicine, blowing smoke and prayers into the bottle. Local allies who have joined this sacred event flank him on both sides.

He calls us up individually. We drink.

For what seems like forever, nothing happens. Well, something…but almost nothing. There's a slight nausea, just enough to keep my attention; a pulsing through my veins; a familiar, uncomfortable feeling—wanting to let go of control but refusing to give it up. The plant scans my body, welcoming me home. The call for drinking more medicine rings out in what seems like the far distance. None for me—the mere thought of drinking another cup is enough to make me purge all on its own.

Streams of reds, electric blues, and yellows cascade between jaguars and snakes and rotating spirals. Intriguing, but nothing life-changing.

Gradually, I begin receiving bits and pieces of information as the plant starts chanting in my ear: "Purge the hate, Nanette, purge the hate." Scenes from my life flash before my eyes amid the mystical animals and swirls. The finger of Mother Nature beckons me to come closer. I'm shown a puma outlined in yellow, then the purging begins. *La Madre* beckons me, "Purge the hate, Nanette. Purge the hate!"

It's pitch dark and my purge bucket is not at my fingertips. I find it just in time, draw it toward my mouth, and violently purge four times. It's horrible and I want it to stop.

The plant reminds me, "We're in this together. You'll be fine."

My response? "*La Madre*, we'll never meet again. I cannot do this."

I hear maniacal laughing. "Oh, we will, my child. We will meet again. Our journey together has just begun."

Soon the ceremony is over. The truth is, I feel lighter.

Otorongo goes back to his room. Chip, Rishi, and I hang out together for a bit, sharing pieces of our journeys.

"I overstand my soul's role in this passion play," Chip says. "We're in for a ride. Yes, *we*—and I don't mean that in the royal sense." We chuckle. "How was your ceremony, Rishi?"

"It was powerful. *La Madre* was kind, yet firm. She showed me many things. I'm not ready to talk about it yet, but I will say this: The doors of my perception have been cleansed."

"I'm scared to open my bucket," I joke. "Demons might come out."

***

"Oh, I love that song!" Lord says as Otorongo sings "Zen Zen *Mariri*[57]" during the ceremony. "I can feel Mother Earth's joy as she works through *Ayahuasca* to heal her children who will, in turn, help heal her. This is so beautiful to witness."

"What is Nanette going to learn?" Gabe asks.

"Mostly she will begin to embrace the fact that her experience of the world as a child was of her mother's hatred and dissatisfaction, nothing more. The protections she had to build and the ways she had to dance to get attention and love are no longer necessary. It is not an easy task to completely rebuild an earthling's foundation. But she is a warrior, with a determined soul. If not, she would have offed herself long ago."

---

[57] Herbert Quinteros, Katari Producciones.

thirty-eight

With ceremony two soon to be underway, we prepare by individually dunking ourselves into a tub of warm water saturated with local flowers and flora. Our flower bath is temperate, fragrant, and connects us more deeply to our surrounding environment. It feels fantastic. We air-dry, put on comfortable clothes, and head toward the ceremony space.

The Second Ceremony

Enrique, one of Otorongo's allies, stands near the door of the temple. He lights the *mapacho*[58] and blows smoke on each side of us, then into the top of our heads. As he finishes, we enter the sacred space cleansed and take our places.

Otorongo sits in front of the circle, meticulously arranging the sacred objects, instruments, and feathers on his *mesa*.[59] A bottle of fresh-brewed *medicina* and a small drinking cup sit in front of him. Next to Otorongo sit Tatiana, his apprentices, and a few guest *curanderos*.[60]

I'm in awe. The perfection of every moment keeps dawning on me.

"Ahora, puedes colocar tus objetos sagrados en el altar."

"You may put your sacred objects on the altar now," Tatiana translates, "if you so desire."

I put a few favorite pieces on the sacred cloth: a wooden beaver figure I found in Alaska, the glass universe—my

---

[58] Jungle tobacco—*Nicotiana rustica*.

[59] In Shamanic terms, a *mesa* is a large cloth that is laid out to hold the shaman's ceremonial items. When not in use, it typically bundles his sacred objects.

[60] Traditional native healers or medicine women or men.

forty-fifth birthday present from G.O.D.—and an elk
jawbone. Rishi deposits an eagle feather, handmade
moccasins, and a significant piece of stone. Chip leaves his
medicine bundle, unopened, on a bed of sage.

As the sun sets, we get settled. Otorongo blows prayers
into the medicine. We sit in silence for several minutes until
Rishi is called forward to drink.

She crawls clockwise around the circle, stopping before
Otorongo. With Tatiana's help, they exchange words and
Otorongo pours her a cup of the thick brown brew. Rishi
drinks, then returns to her seat.

I pass over some sugared ginger slices to help with the
taste. After last night, she's grateful. I had forgotten to bring
them before.

I'm called next.

Otorongo places his hand on my head and blows into my
seventh chakra. My whole head tingles. He pours my
medicine and hands it to me. I say a little prayer, blow into
the thick brew, and drink. It's all I can do not to gag. I take a
piece of sugared ginger and head back to my personal space.

Then Chip drinks. He and Otorongo say a prayer
together, then Chip crawls back to and gets comfortable in
his spot.

La Madre is waiting to continue what she started
yesterday. She wastes no time. Within moments, I've entered
other dimensions, unable to hold on to a thought or pay
attention to anything except my inner world. It is everything I
can do to stop myself from purging too quickly. Time feels as
if it's stopped and sped up all at once.

I can't hold it. I grab my bucket. Bright-colored serpents
dance before my eyes as I let go and purge. The middle of the
room contains a river of souls and spirits, demons, angels,

and animals. I hear, "There is no escaping. I'm in you and out of you."

My body is limp. I couldn't move if I had to.

"Why do I do this to myself?" I ask the ethers for help because I cannot consider getting up.

La Madre assures me, "There is a lot to purge. We will get through this. You will get through this."

Just then, finally, Otorongo starts singing. All at once, I Know exactly what's happening. The medicine is taking me on a journey. She scanned me the first night and is ready to clean me out on the second. Pulsing through my body, wasting no time, I ping-pong between dimensions while doing my best to manage the *hoocha*[61] wanting to come out of both ends. I pray not to shit myself while I'm purging uncontrollably.

"This is the last time we're going to meet," I tell the plant, then dry heave into my bucket. "This is it. Why do I do this to myself?"

"We'll see. You're a warrior, doing what it takes."

All night long, the plant lets me know it's not over. "Just pay attention to what is happening in the present. You'll know exactly what to do, Nanette. And by the way, we will be meeting again."

"Don't be so sure," I say to her as I keep throwing up.

Otorongo finishes an *icaro* and I feel a reprieve, if only for a moment, as if I had the ability to quantify time.

He plays the *charango*.[62]

I purge.

A deep space opens before me in the shape of a vertical tunnel. I peer in from the top. Stairwells flank the sides,

---

[61] Patterns that no longer serve. Dark or dense energy.

[62] Small Andean stringed instrument, a member of the lute family. It's sometimes made from the shell of an armadillo.

rising out of a shallow pool. There are two families with children, one on either side. I see myself on the stairwell on the right, climbing out, about two thirds of the way to the top. Shallow but thick, the bubbly, tar-like substance on the bottom of the shaft reeks of my childhood.

I hear, "You grew up in a pool of hate." The people of my childhood flash before my eyes. "You were poisoned by your mother's anger and vitriol. These feeling are not yours, and you do not have to carry them."

I purge again, once more praying I don't crap on myself. There is no way I can get myself to the bathroom, or even ask for help.

Otorongo comes to my rescue and again blows into my seventh chakra. *"Soplo,"* he says. Old negative forms leave through my hands and feet. I witness The Field receive and transform them, neutralizing their negative impact on the environment and me.

Otorongo shakes a *chakapa*[63] around me, all the while singing, *"Nanettecita, amorcita, allegria in el cuerpo. Medicina, medicina, Abuelita Ayahuasca, limpia, limpia corazón."*[64]

I purge again.

"Limpia, limpia," Otorongo sings. *"Limpia corazón."*

I burst into tears and purge at the same time. The shaman shakes the *chakapa* around me one more time, completing the healing directly in front of my heart.

As he leaves me to go work with Chip, I see a lizard on one side of him and a jaguar on the other. A cricket riding the jaguar's back tells me The Field is having some fun with me.

---

[63] A Quechua word for a shaker or rattle constructed of bundled leaves. Wikipedia.

[64] Loose translation: "Nanette, love, happiness in the body. Medicine, medicine, Grandmother Ayahuasca, clean, clean this heart."

It takes me back to the vision quest I did to celebrate my fortieth birthday.

To prepare for the night alone in the woods, three women and I, guided by a Medicine Woman, journeyed to the lower world to find our power animal. I was led down a beautiful dirt path in the forest, walking, walking, and then I heard noises in the distance. An opening filled with animals appeared on my left. All the creatures you could ever imagine, standing on their haunches in a circle around something in the middle that was not visible to my eye. Once they felt my presence, they parted and bowed toward the middle, each using one of their front paws to guide my attention to the center. It was as if I were watching a lavish stage production and the cast introduced the star. Imagine my surprise and glee when, in the center of the circle, stood a cricket on its hind legs, with its front legs in the air as if it had just won a race.

"The cricket again!" I say to *La Madre*. "Nice touch."

Otorongo sings an *icaro* and the medicine pulses through my body. The Mother speaks. "You've worked long and hard to free yourself from your past. You're to be acknowledged for your perseverance. This hatred is not yours, Nanette, and holding on to any bit of it no longer serves you. You've turned it against yourself for many years. Let go."

After purging for four hours straight, I hope I'm clear. I'm ready for love in this lifetime instead of continually fighting a battle that isn't there.

***

Ceremony two is intense. We all feel the *icaros* drive the medicine and feel the *sonidos de amor*[65] in our bones. As the

---

[65] "Love songs" (literal: "sounds of love").

ceremony comes to an end, Otorongo and his musicians offer
us the sweet sounds of flutes and strings in lighter tunes. The
medicine relaxes its sometimes vicious, but always loving
grip and the visions fade.

"You purged all night," Rishi says.

"The good news is my guts are still intact." I rub my
abdomen lovingly. "Sorry for all the noise."

"I got used to it after a while," she says.

"You've taken purging to a new level," Chip says.
"Can't wait to hear about your journey."

"Last night was...*profundo*. It was difficult and
enlightening all at once. But I don't know if I can do another
night of this... I just don't know. My insides feel raw."

"Isn't every ceremony different, Nanette?" Rishi asks.

"Talk with Otorongo about it," Chip suggests. "He will
guide you."

"Good plan. I think I'll do that right now."

I find Tatiana and ask her to translate for me so I can
have a conversation with Otorongo.

"I'm not sure I want to sit tonight."

Otorongo, sitting on a log chewing a coca leaf, watches
me. He looks at me for what seems like a long time. It's a
little uncomfortable. Then he speaks.

"Listen to me closely," Tatiana translates. "*La Madre*
says she has more to show you. It is up to you to decide. I
cannot tell you what to do. All I can tell you is, she wants
you to know you did the serious work last night. You stepped
into the fire. Tonight, you and the Mother will celebrate.
Celebration is important. But it is up to you."

thirty-nine

Back at the compound, Cretin, Angel, Gil, and Will Gateways enjoy cocktails while keeping tabs on how the weekend's events are playing out across the media on a wall of TVs, each one tuned to a different channel. The same words come out of all the newscasters' mouths.

"Emergency service crews are actively taking care of the convention center," Gil says. "The grounds are being cleared of all non-essential personnel."

"Who planted the bomb?" Cretin asks. "You told me you were simply going to have a threat called in."

"No clue." Gil exudes smugness.

"Not cool," Angel says. "Now we've got to bring our allies together again in another time and at another place. We had an incredible symbiosis happening after the group exercise. We were about to create E.G.O. magic, and it was all over in a flash."

"Literally," Will says.

"E.G.O. magic?" Gil says. "Are you fucking kidding me? This recent turn of events has set the stage for us to strengthen national security and enact more controls, including data mining, media censorship, and the militarization of local governments—all in the name of being 'helpful'! We should be celebrating."

"He's right," Cretin says. "Now we just have to decide who to blame this on."

"The technology is in place," Will says. "It's go time."

"It's press conference time," Gil says, "for broadcast on all networks." He pauses, and then raises a single finger in the air. "Sponsored by Time/Space Corp."

"I've got it," Cretin says. "We'll pin this on a terrorist group calling themselves The G.O.D.—a group sworn to 'becoming your masters.' This couldn't have happened at a better time! America, and perhaps the whole world, is in the palm of our hands. Moving forward, Lord and G.O.D. have no chance of credibility. None! SpirIT, Lord, and his son Chip would be wise to just give up now."

forty

Lord and Gabe enjoy that promised nice dry martini.

"Last night's ceremony was brutal for our girl, but she has so much more to purge than she realizes. It is important for her to sit again tonight. Now that she has seen her past with new eyes, the foundation must be laid for the future."

"It was hard to watch. I understand her reticence. I even overstand it!"

"You can feel her, right, Gabe?"

"I can. The more I get to know her, the more I'm touched by her persistence and continued efforts toward freeing herself from the ties that bind her. What a journey!"

They toast, the clink of the crystal martini glasses echoing into the twilight.

"On another topic," Lord says, "Zephyr and Justine also need our help. Work with Michael and the team to make sure they are safe. Whatever you need to do to make that happen is okay with me." He eats an olive.

"Fantastic! I've been contemplating the most effective way to activate AWE on a grand scale. If Chip sets up a production company on Earth and hires Zephyr to run it, we'll have a channel in place for mass distribution of the laws and the truth. Zephyr has the experience."

Flashing lights on the Map catch Gabe's eye for a second, but it's nothing groundbreaking. "We can keep it on the down low until we're ready to present our first offering. A lot of human beings are already working toward the same goals we are. We'll bring them all together under one umbrella. Enroll them using synchronistic events… Through their own demonstrations, they'll show others and see for themselves the differences between E.G.O.'s made-up God and G.O.D., the real story!"

"What are you waiting for?!" Lord exclaims. "Also, this: From now on, we have to ensure our position on Earth by making sure Team AWE members have everything they need to survive with ease. Pull them out of E.G.O.'s matrix of survival. They cannot be worried about how to feed or house themselves while educating the masses and bringing forth the true reasons for incarnation in a body. The explosion at the convention center is a trigger event that will allow E.G.O. to tighten their controls on the population. We will stand strong and lead by example."

"Time to expose the Powers That Be. E.G.O.'s nerve center revolves around money," Gabe says, "and may be easier to topple than we think. It's the collateral damage we need to watch out for."

forty-one

I spend the rest of the day after the second ceremony sleeping and communing with my master plant, Ushpawasha Sanango. I've followed protocol, drinking about an ounce of the pungent liquid three times a day. I talk with the plant to ask what's happening to me. Is my DNA being rearranged? Am I going to be able to integrate this intense purge? Will I be okay?

"You'll be more than okay," I hear.

Ushpawasha Sanango travels through my body, highlighting all the cleaned spaces. He takes me on a tour of my organs, lighting up each one as he goes, showing me—if only briefly—what freedom feels like. Freedom from the internal hell of battling the two families that have, until now, commanded the space within me.

I was born from a union of love. My biological mother was deeply in love with my father, but they were young and the union couldn't endure. I was placed in a home where I was raised by a woman filled with an endless supply of vitriol. She hated her mother, her friends, her family; she never had anything nice to say about anyone. She loathed the man she married, who, in her eyes, was my biological father. And she took all of that hatred out on the closest targets: my brother Mitchell and me.

Yes, I've got a lot to purge, and I've purged a lot. Feeling a thousand times lighter, I Know, deep in my heart, that I still have work to do. A wave of acknowledgement washes over me as I fall into a deep sleep.

***

After talking with Otorongo, I realize I must participate in this last night of ceremony work. I'm not one to run from the difficult pieces—I usually go headfirst into the flame. But my trepidations about this night's journey are strong and real. I cannot go through another night like last night. *I just can't.*

The Third Ceremony

Darkness falls and the ceremony begins. We're smudged, the directions are invited in, and then we drink.

I gag at the taste of the medicine, but manage to keep it down. Soon after, any desire to purge leaves me.

"Ahh, so we meet again," the plant says to me. She shows me two palms, like human hands, holding four symbols: a heart, a spiral, a thick line next to a circle, and the universe in a globe—exactly like the one I got in Harmony, California, on my forty-fifth birthday.

"I'm a glutton for punishment," I joke. *La Madre* creates bright-colored swirls around me, then shows me fields of beautiful greens and blooming flowers with jaguars, snakes, and beings from many dimensions all dancing together.

"Tonight will be different," she says. "You did the hard work last night. Tonight, we celebrate."

I breathe a sigh of relief and pray that she's not fooling with me. She can be tricky, taking any route necessary to help you with your growth and clearing.

"What is your intention for this ceremony, Nanette?"

"I wish to receive the tools to live and speak from my heart," I answer. "To open its eyes and ears. You've shown me the stronghold my mind has on my perceptions. On my ability to love, to see, to hear. My mind is the filter through which everything enters and exits, alas. The request is for my heart to be my filter instead."

"You have a belief that your heart cannot protect itself, Nanette. That love will always choose from the wrong place. Not true! How sweet and strong LOVE is."

It turns out that on this night, I'm shown what I have. It is not about purging; it is about acknowledgement and acceptance of my gifts.

She tells me, "You have to know what you have, to know what you need." She cleans my lungs of grief, showing me people I've helped throughout the years. She shows me my heart!

"You're a strong and powerful soul, *Hermana*," she says. "There is another piece to healing the hate in your system. A journey."

"What? What kind of journey?"

"You'll see. No more questions."

Just then, as if she sent him over to end the conversation, Otorongo arrives before me and performs a healing. He works on me, singing, "*Curación in el cuerpo, alegria in el cuerpo, felicidad in el cuerpo,*"[66] over and over.

Through Tatiana, he tells me my solar plexus is shut down. He says I need to have a relationship with it, with power, with the sun, and with fire. He tells me my masculine needs tending.

I understand his message on a deep level. I felt my solar plexus slam shut that day many years ago when I found out my birth father had died.

I contemplate my masculine needing attention and ask for guidance from the plant. Before the ceremony is over, I receive one more teaching, about masculine and feminine.

---

[66] Loose translation: "Recovery/healing in the body, joy in the body, happiness in the body."

I've felt for some time that the feminine side of me is weak and needs to be strengthened in order to blossom.

La Madre shows me it's not weak. In fact, it's overworked.

She tells me my feminine side has been overcompensating for an underdeveloped masculine side. It's time to allow the feminine to rest…give her a break. Allow the masculine a voice.

The night comes to an end and candles are lit to illuminate the space.

Otorongo plays a sweet song on the *charango* and his friends join in with drums and flutes. I can still feel sensations of the medicine coming in spurts, but it's clear the evening's necessary work is complete.

Chip and Rishi come over to my blanket and we all hug. "Let's download tomorrow," he says.

I head to the kitchen for some chilled fresh ripe cherries, then to my room for some sweet deep sleep.

***

Morning arrives, and with the rise of the sun, Otorongo and Tatiana say their goodbyes. We're so grateful to them for the work done together over the past week.

"Recuerda de seguir la dieta por otros siete días. Es importante."

"Remember to stick to the diet for seven more days. It's important."

"Message received, Otorongo," I say.

"Mensaje recibido," Tatiana offers. "We'll arrange a time for your Spanish lessons!" She kisses me on the forehead.

We bid them farewell, then sit down to talk about our experiences.

Rishi says, "I saw the world after the destruction being repopulated with living things. It was magical. Life-forms dropped from the sky in large raindrop carriages. They broke open when they hit the Earth and some new creature would scamper into the dense forest."

"The destruction. Hmm," Chip says. "Could be a metaphor for the end of E.G.O."

"I purged a great deal of energetic *hoocha*," I say. "And I saw the pool of hatred I grew up in. How much I've climbed out of! And how much farther I have to go... There's something about being witnessed by all of nature that brings a depth to my understanding. I would even call it an overstanding now. I'm no longer seeing my experiences from the little picture."

"So you're saying you still have work to do?" Chip asks.

"Yes, and *La Madre* said something about a journey. I don't know."

Rishi offers, "Sounds as if you need to be open. You've always been good at rolling with the punches."

"Chip, how about you? What wisdom did you receive from your journey?" I ask.

"I was shown truths about the state of affairs on the planet and learned what it's going to take to shift the masses to a state of reality. Our work is cut out for us, Nanette. And Rishi, you're a part of this as well. It's good we've got each other for support. Our road seems long, but it widens with every person who wakes up and begins demonstrating truth and teaching others. Human beings learn by example. And demonstration of principles will win over words every time."

"Anything more specific? I want details."

"Well, there are a lot more specifics, but I've been advised that for now, the information I received is only for me. The unfolding of truth and your part in it will come when you're ready. You're still working on your own issues."

"Wheee!" I throw my arms around Rishi. "I'm giddy because we're in this together! At least I won't be called crazy alone." She hugs me and we burst out laughing. *What an incredible life!*

"We'll leave in the morning," Chip says. "How would you like to spend the afternoon?"

"We have many moons to be together," I say. "I would like to spend time alone with the trees and Earth, paying reverence to my plant companions on this journey. They're requesting silence so I can continue to receive their teachings."

"And you, Rishi?" Chip asks.

"What are you doing?" she asks him.

"I'm going to sit down by the stream. You're both welcome to join me at any time."

"Thanks," she answers. "I'm not sure."

forty-two

"We've got to throw the public a bone," Cretin says to Angel when they're finally alone together after a couple of long and arduous weeks.

"What do you think it should be?"

"The disbelievers," he says. "We've got to distract their attention from their narrowing band of rights and the nullifying of constitutional policy. Focus their thoughts on something that'll make them feel all warm and fuzzy. The staunch believers will stay with us, even if we piss them off, but we have to give the undecideds something to occupy their minds and direct their energies to. This'll be good for everyone!"

"Whatcha thinkin', big guy?" Angel purrs and runs her fingers through his fluffy troll hair, evoking a playful gurgle/growl. "You know it really turns me on when you formulate massive control ideologies."

"Let's reintroduce a ban on gay marriage and marijuana. How's that for a strategy?"

"Either one, honey—or both! That'll keep 'em all busy."

Cretin kisses her. "This is going to be fun. It's good to be the puppet master."

"Oh, Cretin," she says, "yes, it is. Lord doesn't stand a chance."

***

"Are you ready?"

"For what, Lord?" Gabe asks.

"Your trip to Earth to set up the office."

"Really? Now? That's a surprise!" Gabe takes a second to program a sunrise.

"Be prepared for spur-of-the-moment anything." The overseer quickly throws his hands toward Gabe, startling him a bit.

"Point taken. Did they get an office? What about Nanette's journey?"

"All will be revealed to you when you need the knowledge, Gabriel. Prepare yourself—choose your human skin, gather your tools. It is now your responsibility to find and rent a suitable location, and set up CPR ~ Earth. Everything you need will be provided."

Excited and nervous, Gabe runs off to prepare for his trip. "What an adventure! I'll be ready in a jiffy."

***

"Got everything?" Chip asks as Rishi and I simultaneously arrive at the car.

"I say yes with a heavy heart." I get down on my haunches and rub my palms in the dirt. "God, I love this place." They both agree.

We ride home mostly in silence. Rishi gets dropped off first. Upon arrival at my home, my landlord, David, is waiting for me. "Can I talk with you privately?"

Chip takes the cue and walks around back.

"I've got some, uh, news. Let me start with 'I'm so sorry,' and don't worry, the cat's fine."

"Sorry about what?" I was happy to hear about the cat. David watches her for me when I'm away.

"You have to move. We're getting divorced."

"Huh?"

He starts crying. I don't know whether to console him or myself. It's difficult to take care of someone else's emotions when they're kicking you out of what's been your home for the last ten years.

Composing himself, he says, "You can have sixty days if you need it, but thirty days would be appreciated. We need to separate as soon as possible. One of us will be moving into your place. Thanks for your understanding."

"I hate it when people thank me for something I don't have," I deadpan after I tell Chip what's happening.

Chip checks in. SpirIT plays a few notes on a tenor sax, tuning him so he knows exactly what to say.

A hummingbird flies by.

"Rejoice, Nanette. Mother *Ayahuasca's* prophecy is already here. You're going on a journey!"

"I'm not quite there yet. I have no idea what to do."

I sit on a lounge chair, resting my elbows on my thighs and my chin on my palms.

"Remember that you're never alone," he says. "You have many allies, including Lord and The Field." Olivia walks by and drags her tail across my leg. "Now is the most important time to practice demonstrating what you've learned—and it's the easiest time to forget and fall back into old patterns."

I pull Chip in close and squeeze. "I need time to integrate all these recent events. I've got a lot to figure out. I know 'I'm never alone' and that I'm being guided, but sometimes it feels so much the opposite. I'm not sure I know how to do that. I need a nap. Talk later?"

"Sweet dreams, Sunshine. I'll see you soon. And by the way, my dear one, you have been received."

***

"So she is being forced into a journey."

"Yes, Lord," Chip says. "I wonder what SpirIT has in mind for her."

"This is fantastic." Lord brings his hands together in a big clap and squeezes them together. "All she has to do is listen and follow the subtle Field Prompts and she will learn everything she needs to know to be the cause of change on Earth. By the way, keep an eye out for Gabe. He is headed your way.

"Earth skin?" Chip asks.

"He has not shown me, but do not worry. You two will recognize each other."

***

Gabe lands somewhere in Los Angeles, having decided to arrive as a woman."

"Hi, I'm Gabriella," she says to the person next to her. "Can you direct me to Santa Monica?"

"Don't you have GPS?" the person says rudely and keeps going.

"Oh, yeah," she says, not fazed in the least. She looks at her watch, a mini Sheet of the World, and transports herself to exactly where she wants to be—the beach.

"I'll just take a break before getting started."

She checks in with CPR.

"Gabriella?" Lord says. "Nice. It is perfect that you are a woman. Let the adventure begin."

And with that, everything is set in motion.

Welcome to the future.

EPILOGUE

Nanette, forgetting everything she just learned about listening and Field Prompts, is in a tizzy trying to figure out what to do, where to go, and how to assimilate all this.

Just then, the phone rings.

"Hello?"

"Hey, Nanette. Have you found a place to live yet?"

THE END

GLOSSARY OF TERMS

acronyms

AID (v): Acknowledgement In Demonstration

ASK/GET (v): Always Seek Knowing, Gain Eternal Truths, aka the law of ASK/GET

AWE (n): Awakened Weavers ~ Earth, aka Team AWE

CHIP (n): Contact Higher Inner Powers

CLUES (n): Cryptic Lessons Unleashing Everyday Secrets

CPR (n): Center Presenting Reality, aka the Center, headquarters of the G.O.D.

CPR ~ EARTH (n): Center Presenting Reality ~ Earth Branch

E.G.O. (n): Elite Global Order

EAT (n): Edible Alternative Technology

EWE (n): E.G.O's Workers ~ Earth, aka EWE's Army

FIELD, The (n): Frequency In Earth's Linear Dimension, aka The Field of Awareness

FLOW (v): Fluidity Lets Order Work

G.O.D. (n): Galactic Order of Demonstration

GROW (v): Giving Receptivity Opens Worlds

HOME LAW BOOK (n): Heaven On Mother Earth Law Book, the; aka the Book of Laws

IT (n): SpirIT's nickname, stands for I Tune.

LOVE (n): Lens Opening Virtually Everything

LOVE (v): Listening Opens Vibratory Evolution.

LOVE FIELD (n): Lens Opening Virtually Every Frequency In Earth's Linear Dimension

PRACTICE (v): Pure Ritual Acts Culminate Teachings Invoking Conscious Expansion

PROJECT FF (n): E.G.O.'s Fight or Flight initiative to keep all earthlings in perpetual defense mode

TASTE (n): Technical Autocratic Slave Tenure Enacted
THEY (n): Time Honored Earth Yentas
WAR (n): We Are Right
WAVE (v): Whispers Aligning Virtually Everything

words

"Play The Field": Slogan for The G.O.D. to encourage
    earthlings to realize they've been fed lies and need to
    learn the truth.
"Weaving Spiders Don't Come Here" (idiom): The
    Bohemian Grove's rule about not "spinning the future"
    or doing business during the annual summer event.
Akashic records (n): The Library of Eternity, where
    everything that has ever happened, is happening, or will
    happen is recorded, aka the Hall of Records.
AWE-Wakening (n): G.O.D.'s name for the new wave of
    overstanding they're heralding on the Earth, aka AWE-
    wakening, aka AWE-waken.
Bible (n): E.G.O.'s construction, based on the HOME Law
    Book, to control the masses and forward their agenda.
Big War (n): What Cretin calls the bet between E.G.O. and
    G.O.D.; aka the longest game of Earthopoly in the
    history of G.O.D.
Bohemian Grove, The (n): aka The Grove, E.G.O.'s highly
    guarded meeting place where they hold their annual get-
    togethers.
Bohemians (n): Elite Global Order's most powerful
    members.
Clue of the Obstacle (n): The thing you think is in the way of
    your path, is your path. With this appreciation comes the
    Clue of Obstacle.

Consciousness Competency Testing (v): G.O.D.'s system for checking a soul for listening and following Field directives.

Cremation of Care Ceremony (n): E.G.O. ceremony, aka Cremation of Care.

Crypt of Dull Care (n): aka Dull Care, aka Care, feminine.

demonstrate (v): Take action and demonstrably show your love, passion, understanding, knowledge, and gifts.

demonstration (n): The action taken. The result of an earthling's demonstrating (v). Demonstration sends a message to The Field that you are listening, and is the only prayer.

Demonstration Cycle (n): Interacting with The Field regarding a previous lesson and assimilating the knowledge gained.

dieta (n): The way one eats to prepare for plant ceremonies.

Earth (n): Our planet, feminine.

Earth's Demonstration Game (n): Asking the right questions, translating the clues, and acting on the guidance of The Field, aka paying attention, allowing, and acting accordingly.

earthlings (n): General name for the population, no matter which side they're on.

EGOtised/EGOtising (v): Elite Global Order's propaganda delivery system; propaganda delivered as advertising.

EWE's Army (n): E.G.O.'s Workers ~ Earth, the team that carries out Lucifer, Cretin, and Gil's wishes.

faklempt (adj) (Yiddish): "Beside yourself."

Field Prompts (n): aka Universal Field Directives: Communication system between The Field, earthlings, and human beings.

Galactic Advancement (n): Achieving completion in the Galactic Order of Demonstration, then moving on to the next order.

Galactic Field (n): aka The Field, the interactive container we live in.

Galactic Order of Demonstration (n): The interactive Field we live in. Also known as the G.O.D.

Galactic Orders (n): Souls move through these to gain much-needed wisdom. There are seven: (1) mission retrieval, (2) soul development, (3) ethics, (4) giving and receiving, (5) demonstration (of overstandings of all the previous missions—souls can go either backward or forward from here), (6) relaxation, (7) Galactic Order of the Next Cosmos education.

Global Corporate Citizenship (n): Buzz words using doublespeak to claim corporations join together to put the betterment of local communities and the people over the accumulation of profits.

Great Mystery (n): aka *el misterio*—birth, life, death, spirit, and the meaning of it all.

grokking (v): Knowing on an innate basis.

Holo-Deck (n): Transportation system utilizing physics to transport people between places without them physically having to leave where they are.

HU (n): The vibration man aligns with to become Human.

HU-man (n): G.O.D. man.

Human beings (n): Earthlings who have learned the truth of G.O.D. and the way the place really works.

icaros (n) (Quechua: *ikaro*): A song sung or whistled in healing ceremonies. They are used to enhance or subdue the effects of plant medicines, to evoke plant spirits, to invite the spirits of others or the deceased, to dispel dark spirits, or to protect those present, and to manage the ceremony.

incarnate (n): A soul, in the body it has taken on, who lives on Earth.

indranet (n): Cosmic communication system available for use by anyone InFlow, aka the jeweled web. SpirIT uses it to tune, communicate with, and deliver Field Prompts to earthlings.

InFlow (n): The term used to describe following G.O.D.'s universal laws of demonstration, or operating in alignment with The Field.

Knowing (v): Innate, intuitive Knowledge that doesn't have to be learned.

kvelling (v) (Yiddish): So excited about something.

La Madre Ayahuasca (n): *Ayahuasca* is an Amazonian plant mixture that is capable of inducing altered states of consciousness, usually lasting between 4–8 hours after ingestion. Ranging from mildly stimulating to extremely visionary, *Ayahuasca* is used primarily as a medicine and as a Shamanic means of communication, typically in a ceremonial session under the guidance of an experienced drinker. http://www.ayahuasca-info.com/introduction

mango toast (n): A piece of sourdough bread, slathered with creamery butter and smothered with ripe, fresh cut mango slices.

MEMEMEbook (n): EGOcentric website.

nudgings (n): Hints from The Field.

opening (v): Allowing yourself to receive.

Oracle, the (n): aka Lakshmi.

overstander (n): Someone who gets the big picture.

overstanding (v): Grokking the big picture.

Owl of Bohemia (n): 40-foot concrete and wire statue at The Grove, aka the Great Owl; is considered a god for E.G.O., aka Bohemia.

puppets (n): Earthlings who are potential humans, fossilized in an intricate web of misdirection.

Seven Attunements of Demonstration (n): Ask, Accept,
    Allow, Assimilate, Acknowledge, Appreciate, Awe.
Sheet of the World (n): aka the Map, created by Gabe for
    G.O.D. for tracking Earth denizens.
SpirIT (n): Source Power Invoking Resonance ~ I Tune, aka
    Great SpirIT, aka Great One.
synchronicity (n): Confirmation of someone following Field
    Prompts.
TASTE Conference (n): E.G.O.'s name for this year's annual
    convention.
Team AWE (n): AWEs on Earth.
Team AWE Broadcasting (n): How the Map alerts and
    communicates with AWEs, aka the Team AWE
    Broadcasting system.
transceiver (n): Something that transmits and receives.
tuning fodder (n): Any communication from SpirIT to
    earthlings through Field Prompts, signs, divine inner
    Knowings, etc.
understanding (v): Grokking the details of a piece of the big
    picture.
Virtual Vision Viewers (n): Hand-sized computer attached to
    glasses that give users immediate access to a wide range
    of information.
Voice of E.G.O. (n): The ruling power's system of telling
    you what to do, how you should live, and who to give
    your money to, all orchestrated through E.G.O.'s rules
    called laws and earthling's unquestioning compliance.
Voice of The Field (n): G.O.D.'s universal laws revealed
    through Field Prompts.

ACKNOWLEDGEMENTS

The toughest thing about writing this book was moving forward when my enthusiasm waned. Many people along the way offered kind words and encouragement that helped me cross the finish line.

Deep love and appreciation to Dena Plotkin, Diane Amos, Barbara Deutsch, John Guidry, Greg Berke, Libby Fountain, Lori Kaplan, Darcy Lubbers, Robin Miller, Deborah Wakeham, Rosa Diaz, Craig Swogger, Tracey Bleahu, Tricia Bowler, Sage Justice, Frankie Colmane, Laura Hippiechick, Vicki Baldwin, Robert Berger, Keely Berger, Minda Burr, Billy Biegler, Martin Ngo, and all my Jesuits! To Ryan Cramer for the use of MS Word. To Ron Lindbloom and Donna Schoefield Putney for celebrating milestones with me. I would also like to thank my teachers, Roger Weir and Dr. Vernon Wolfe.

Some of you took time out of your busy lives to read pre-edited versions, brainstorm with me, and/or provide feedback. I am in awe of you, especially after cutting sixty pages! To Ira Knox, Nancy Falkner, Jessica Porter, Cheyenne Kowal, Carrie Vandenberg, April Shicker, Olivia Bareham, Julie Coren, Anita Byrd, Kim Randolph, Robin Gilbert Harris Kanoff, Amy Fukuizumi, Laurel Eisenschiml and my brother, Mitchell Glin: Thank you is anemic to describe my gratitude.

Special thanks to Oracle Tatiana Heimberger-Boza for reading the Tarot Cards and offering her insights. And to Bobo and Pietro at Piccolo in Los Angeles for the *Cena de Quattro* menu. Another shout-out to Carrie V. for braving the sweetbreads with me.

Amy Nanette Glin

This book is about allowing yourself to be guided by The Field. I'm convinced that my editor, Susan Uttendorfsky, was sent via SpirIT. Thank you, Susan, for a master class in writing, passionate and thoughtful editing, and for your unending professionalism peppered with just the right amount of sass! I am beyond grateful.

ABOUT THE AUTHOR

Amy Nanette Glin is a resilient soul passionate about storytelling, personal growth, and shaking up the status quo.

Convinced that there's more to life than what we're led to believe, Amy followed an unconventional path, including moving over 70 times since she was 18, working in a rock-n-roll nightclub, managing comedians, creating products, cooking for celebrities and Jesuit priests and working with individuals to help them identify and change the beliefs that don't serve them.

Following the call of SpirIT, Amy spent the last year traveling around the Pacific Northwest, pet-sitting for cats, dogs, reptiles, farm animals, and a tortoise. For now, she has landed in Portland, Oregon. She's listening for the next directive from The Field to see where life will take her.

www.ingramcontent.com/pod-product-compliance
Lightning Source LLC
Chambersburg PA
CBHW030405130626
46549CB00004B/1639